DEFEND
THE BORDER &
SAVE LIVES

DEFEND
THE BORDER &
SAVE LIVES

SOLVING OUR MOST IMPORTANT HUMANITARIAN AND SECURITY CRISIS

TOM HOMAN

CENTER
STREET.

NEW YORK   NASHVILLE

Center Street
Hachette Book Group
1290 Avenue of the Americas, New York, NY 10104
centerstreet.com
twitter.com/centerstreet

First Edition: March 2020

Center Street is a division of Hachette Book Group, Inc. The Center Street name and logo are trademarks of Hachette Book Group, Inc.

The publisher is not responsible for websites (or their content) that are not owned by the publisher.

This book reflects the author's present recollections of experiences over time. Some dialogue has been recreated.

Print book interior design by Timothy Shaner, NightandDayDesign.biz

Library of Congress Cataloging-in-Publication Data has been applied for.

ISBNs: 978-1-5460-8593-5 (hardcover), 978-1-5460-8594-2 (ebook)

Printed in the United States of America

LSC-C

10 9 8 7 6 5 4 3 2 1

DEDICATION

I wish to dedicate this book to the fallen Border Patrol agents and the fallen ICE officers and special agents, including those who fell serving their legacy agencies, the US Customs Service and the US Immigration and Naturalization Service. These brave men and women made the ultimate sacrifice for this great nation, and we must never forget them. Their hearts stopped beating while protecting this nation—standing between us and lawlessness. They left the safety and security of their homes, armed themselves, enforced the laws they took an oath to enforce, and kept Americans safe.

I also dedicate this book to the families of these brave souls. They have also made a profound sacrifice for this country. Family members may not have worn the uniform, but they served every day that their loved ones served.

Further, I dedicate this book to the men and women in law enforcement who continue to serve today—not only at ICE and the Border Patrol but every federal, state, and local law enforcement officer out there. The agents and officers put themselves in harm's way every time they report to duty. These moms, dads, sons, daughters, sisters, and brothers face the danger when others flee. They defend those who cannot defend themselves and even protect those who despise them. They will face adversity and attacks from many—including from some elected officials. Regardless, when the next shift starts, they will be there holding the line and protecting others.

God Bless them all.

CONTENTS

AUTHOR'S NOTE

Readers will notice my use of the term *illegal alien* in this book. In today's conversation on immigration, this term has been labeled by some as derogatory. That is certainly not my intent, and I think a review of this book will set the record straight that I have spent my entire career saving lives and protecting those that are most vulnerable while enforcing the laws as written. It is more a "term of art," with a precise, specialized meaning within the profession of immigration enforcement. The term *illegal alien* has been interchanged many times with the term *illegal immigrant*, but that is often inaccurate as the terms *alien* and *immigrant* are separately defined in federal statute, specifically within Title 8 of the United States Code, and are not always interchangeable.

ONE

WHO I FIGHT FOR

There were 4,158 child exploitation cases initiated in 2018,
and 1,588 criminal arrests for human trafficking.
—2018 HOMELAND SECURITY INVESTIGATIONS

31.4 percent of women and 17.2 percent of men have been sexually
abused during their journey to the United States' border.
—2017 DOCTORS WITHOUT BORDERS REPORT

During my law enforcement career, which spans over three decades, I was part of a team of men and women who were deeply respected. Most Americans acknowledged the job as necessary and dangerous. But in the past few years, I've been labeled as heartless, a racist, and even a Nazi—and that's just by some Democrats in Congress.

Human traffickers, drug dealers, and criminals of all types never called me such names. I've arrested thousands of illegal aliens, and the vast majority of them respected the power of the badge because they knew we had an army of badges. Many actually feared the badge because they were so accustomed to police corruption in their homeland.

Whether people realize it or not, every country and every community depends on a clear set of laws and the brave people who help enforce the law. It's on behalf of those amazing men and women—local, state, and federal—that I offer my perspective on the most pressing issues facing the United States: border security, public safety, and immigration.

But it's not only about the law; it's really about what—and who—the law protects.

HOMELAND SECURITY

In early 2003, the Department of Homeland Security (DHS) was created along with Immigration and Customs Enforcement (ICE). This department and agency were established because of the terror attacks of September 11, 2001, given that many of the perpetrators were in this country illegally. Our citizens wanted to better secure our borders and enforce our nation's immigration laws. ICE was created out of the legacy US Immigration and Naturalization Service (INS) law enforcement components and the legacy US Customs (USC) law enforcement component. Sorry to give you four acronyms in one paragraph, but it gives you a sense of the challenge I was up against—helping the two legacy agencies transition into the new, post-9/11 world.

In March 2003, I was sent to Washington, DC, as part of a team transitioning and creating the agencies—and frankly, trying to make sense of it all. You can't imagine the tangle of policies and personnel involved. I'll spare you the details, but there was much distrust between the personnel of both agencies and a lot of jockeying for power. It was a very tense time. However, we tried to make it work because, at this point in our nation, combining two border law enforcement agencies into one was the right thing to do.

While on extended detail to ICE headquarters in DC, I was asked to travel to Dallas on May 13 to join Bob Wallis, who was the acting special agent in charge, at the time. Yes, we like acronyms and refer to that title as SAC. Bob Wallis was a legacy INS senior leader and also my longtime mentor. At one point in his career, he was the leader of one third of the Immigration and Naturalization Service. It was a huge job, and he was good at it. I was most excited about the trip because it was another chance to see my wife and kids. Dallas was my home station, and I'd been on detail to DC for several months, able to return home only every couple of weeks.

Bob and I were there to give a speech to the International Association of Chiefs of Police, trying to explain what DHS and ICE were, and how this new agency would work with local law enforcement. On the first day of the conference our cell phones began to light up during our presentation. At first, we ignored the calls and tried to focus on our talk for a few minutes, but they kept coming—and were from a Washington, DC, area code. Something was wrong. We excused ourselves and called HQ.

There had been a deadly human smuggling incident in Victoria, Texas, and media were already swarming the scene. Because of my experience in human trafficking investigations I was directed by the new ICE director, Michael Garcia, to immediately deploy to the crime scene. Bob was also directed to accompany me because of his reputation for handling international incidents. He oversaw the widely publicized Elian Gonzalez international custody battle in 2000. We didn't know much about the crime, but we knew this would be a crucial test for a brand-new agency. Our response would make or break us. As our first large-scale case, it was imperative that we work quickly and effectively. Failure was not an option. The eyes of the entire nation were on us—including those in the Oval Office of the White House.

With only the clothes on our backs, Bob Wallis and I flew down to the crime scene on a small Air and Marine plane from Love Field in Dallas. Bob was to handle all media and communication and serve as the senior official on the scene. I was to oversee the investigative operation and incident response. I was fine with this plan since I'd spent a major portion of my time as a special agent investigating and prosecuting alien smuggling and human trafficking organizations in Phoenix, Arizona. And I learned from one of the best, Armando Garcia, who recently retired as an assistant special agent in charge (ASAC) in Phoenix and remains a dear friend to this day.

In Victoria, Texas, we were picked up by special agents from ICE and driven to the site of the incident. We noticed multiple media outlets trying to capture video, and we were warned that the scene was horrific—multiple dead bodies in a tractor trailer. State and local law enforcement were there, along with fire crews, attempting to shield the site from view. The county sheriffs quickly escorted me into the crime scene. The looks on their faces told me to prepare for the worst. Even after thirty years in law enforcement, I was not prepared for what I saw.

THE TRUE COST OF CHAOS

As we stood before the open doors of the tractor trailer, I couldn't believe my eyes. Seventeen dead bodies lay inside on the hot metal floor and on the ground outside the open doors. A total of nineteen people died—seventeen were dead at the scene, and two died on the way to the hospital. We learned that the bodies on the ground had been piled up near the doors. When the doors were finally opened, several victims fell to the ground. Then, as more than fifty survivors rushed out to get air, they knocked more bodies out of the way. I tried to survey the scene as an investigator. Most of the dead were stripped down to just their underwear in an apparent attempt to get relief from the extreme heat.

I jumped up into the trailer with an ICE photographer and stood there for several minutes. "Oh my God. Oh my God," I stammered.

Even with the doors open it was unbearably hot in that steel box. My eyes were quickly drawn to the body of a small boy who was wearing yellow underwear and lying on his stomach. He seemed to be about the same age and size as my youngest son. His body had already started to discolor with livor mortis (lividity), bluish-purple discoloration in the lowest part of the body. Investigators and coroners use the images of this discoloration to help ascertain the time and cause of death. The color was most noticeable on his tiny face. I could tell he'd been dead for hours. I slowly walked around the dead bodies and instructed the photographer about the pictures I needed, intentionally avoiding the small boy.

Every time I glanced at the child, an overwhelming sense of anxiety came over me—not only because of the horrific scene, but because he so reminded me of my own son. After we had all the other photos, we finally approached the boy, who was lying partially under the collapsed body of a man who we learned was his father. It appeared that the father was embracing and comforting his son at the time of his death. Several survivors later testified that this innocent little boy was the first to perish, crying "Daddy, Daddy, I'm dying." I knelt down and put my hand on his small head, and I prayed for him.

I somehow kept my composure but was an emotional mess inside. After a few moments I stood back up, looked at the photographer, who was also visibly shaken, and asked him to take pictures of that small child. I wanted those pictures to be seen by the special agents working the case, the prosecutors, the media, those in the court, and the jury. I wanted everyone to see what I saw so they would show no mercy to the people responsible for these murders. Hence, the investigation was called Operation No Mercy.

I spent the next several hours combing through the crime scene with the photographer, who I told to "take pictures of everything" even though the local sheriff's team had already photographed the area. As we surveyed the scene and interviewed survivors, the true horror of the scene became painfully obvious. Bodies were piled up near the back of the truck in a desperate attempt to find fresh air around the locked doors. The suffocating passengers broke out some brake lights to create ventilation. Many appeared to have died in the struggle to breathe. It was estimated that the temperature reached as high as 173 degrees inside.

I will never forget the scene, the thought of what these people endured, and what must have been their excruciating final minutes of life. It's still fresh in my mind, and when I tell the story I still get choked up. I can still smell it, taste it, see it. Tears fill my eyes as I write this.

HEARTBREAK TO ANGER

That night, when I finally arrived at a hotel, I called my wife and tried to convey the experience. I couldn't get the images out of my mind—the expressions of agony and fear on the lifeless faces. As a border patrol agent, I'd seen death before, but nothing like this. Their contorted bodies barely looked human.

I couldn't sleep that night or for the next three nights. Every time I closed my eyes, my mind was flooded with memories of the scene. *What if that was my young son in the trailer? What if I was in there with him?*

I imagined what the father must have thought: *I did this to us. I put us in this situation. I killed my little boy!* But I couldn't imagine hearing the cries of my five-year-old as he collapsed in my arms.

Let's be clear. This was not a "tragedy." This was mass murder. These people didn't have to die. Stories like this have become so commonplace that our reaction is often to mutter, "How sad," and move on to the next crisis. Unless you've stepped through a crime scene with seventeen dead bodies, you cannot fathom the deep horror. We know how uncomfortable it is to be in a hot car in the summer. Imagine being in that car but unable to unlock the doors, open a window, or turn on the air-conditioning. You are locked in a metal box. An oven. After an hour you can't swallow because you have no fluid left in you. Your nostrils burn every time you breathe, and every breath becomes more pointless. The trailer was so packed, it was standing room only. It was a nightmare, and these people experienced their death in slow motion.

Even though I'd been a cop and border patrol agent for almost two decades, this experience made Tom Homan who he is today. Don't let anyone tell you that illegal immigration is a victimless crime. Our crisis on the border is actually hundreds of crises and crimes—every single day.

The more we learned about this human smuggling operation, the more my sorrow intensified and turned to burning anger. We had to find the people responsible for these deaths. US Attorney Michael Shelby, probably the most talented US attorney I've met in my career, immediately joined us and declared that everyone responsible for this would be held accountable. I called ICE headquarters and told them we needed agents. We worked very closely with the sheriff's department, the Texas Rangers, and Customs and Border Protection. We had agents assigned in all the major surrounding cities because we knew there were different branches of the trafficking organization. It was all hands on deck, and we hit hard. The Houston field office was ground zero and had many talented agents. One particular agent was Marc Sanders, a smart investigator who knew exactly what needed to be done.

Within weeks, fourteen people were arrested, including the driver of the truck, who had abandoned the scene. During the criminal proceedings, we learned that the driver was paid $7,500 by smugglers to transport the human cargo. The rendezvous point was changed to a location two hundred miles farther. He heard the people banging on the doors and pulled over to see what was going on. After slipping a few bottles of water through an opening the desperate passengers had created, he drove on toward the meeting place, ignoring their screams for help.

He then called the smugglers and demanded more money because of the damage to his rig. At a rest stop, he was spotted putting more water bottles through holes in the trailer. The driver opened the back doors, saw several dead bodies fall onto the pavement, unhooked the trailer, and sped away. According to the ruling by the US Court of Appeals for the Fifth Circuit, "There were several dead bodies on the ground by the trailer doors. Bodies, both dead and living, were stacked in a pile in the trailer. Some of the aliens were standing behind the pile. The aliens were stripped down to their underwear and were sweating. They had clawed at the foam on the inside of the trailer, and the trailer smelled of vomit, urine, feces, and blood."

FOR JOSE AND MARCO

I left out one important detail from the first day of the investigation. Once all the bodies were bagged at the crime scene and the photography was complete, we hired a tow truck to hook up to the trailer. We needed to move the trailer but also wanted to test the air-conditioning system to see if it worked. Shock turned to disbelief as cool air began to flood into the steel box where seventeen people died.

The driver had turned the cooling system off to evade suspicion at truck checkpoints.

As I watched the coroners tag and carry away the stiffened corpses, I was struck by the fact that these were human beings, but their hearts weren't beating and their lungs weren't breathing.

Nineteen people were murdered, including Jose and Marco, the father and son who perished in each other's arms. All this misery and death happened because criminals wanted to make money.

If you saw what I saw that day, you would understand why I'm so emotional about border security, illegal immigration, and national policy. This story is just one example of the preventable human cost of the chaos—created, then ignored, by politicians and special-interest groups. Unspeakable horrors like this are not what legal immigration is about—this is organized crime, operating within our country.

Don't tell me you care about immigrants and yet want to do nothing to stop human smuggling—and nothing to support the men and women of law enforcement who go after these criminals. There's a crisis, but a solution is possible. We want law and order on our streets and in our communities, so why is there even controversy about having law and order at our border? There is no downside to securing our border. There is no downside to fewer illegal drugs pouring into our country. There is no downside to less human smuggling, and there is certainly no downside to taking dollars away from criminal cartels—the same cartels that have murdered our agents and officers.

We are a sovereign country and have every right to protect our borders, because not everyone crossing that border is coming here to have a better life. Some will be smuggling drugs, some will be smuggling guns, some are coming here to terrorize neighborhoods for profit. The reason you have locks and alarms on your home is the same reason we should have locks and alarms on the southern border. Secure borders save lives. Isn't that reason enough?

Secure borders strangle human smugglers, drug traffickers, and cartels. Secure borders create secure communities. That's what this battle on the border is all about.

STOLEN MITTENS

When you grow up with a sense of community, you want everyone to have the same experience.

From the moment I first walked that Victoria crime scene, and for the many weeks that followed, I couldn't help but wonder, *What brought these victims to the point that they risked so much? Why did that little boy's safety and life have to be on the line?*

I was also pondering questions about my own life. *How was I so fortunate to be born in a country that was so rich with opportunities? Why did I have such a great childhood and never have to cope with the struggles these victims had. Was it luck?*

I grew up in the small town of West Carthage, New York. The population was probably no more than two thousand people—a small village, really—and located about six miles from Fort Drum. At the time, Fort Drum was a large military training camp. West Carthage was, and still is, a very patriotic community. Most people worked at one of the nearby paper mills, at Fort Drum, or on small family farms.

My parents had seven kids, two boys and five girls. Our upbringing was very conservative and very Catholic. We went to mass every

Sunday and sat in the same pew every time. God help anyone who arrived before us and sat in our seats! My father was a World War II hero who was awarded two Purple Hearts and a Bronze Star with an Oak Leaf Cluster, which symbolizes a second Bronze Star, but he never talked about his experience in the Pacific much. He worked at Fort Drum but also was a police officer, and he later became a local magistrate, which is what judges were called in our community. My mom, for most of my childhood, was a stay-at-home mom. I remember her always being in the kitchen or doing laundry, and she always wore an apron. With that many kids, there were plenty of mouths to feed and dirty clothes. As a little boy, I distinctly remember that her apron was usually damp from doing dishes or laundry, and it always smelled like soap. She was a loving mom. My dad was tough and not very high on the affection scale, but my mom showed enough affection for both of them. Don't get me wrong—my dad loved his family greatly and put his love into action every day, so we could have what he never had. In high school, I competed in the wrestling program, and no matter how far I had to travel across the state for the match, my dad was always in the stands.

I never met my grandfather Homan. He died when I was a baby, but I always heard about his life as a police officer in our town. I still have his police whistle and well-worn paperback notebook, which was given to me when I followed in his footsteps. Because I never knew him, I treasure that notebook with its handwritten records of his police activities. And his writings are also stirring because they point to a time and place in America that too few of us have experienced.

One of my favorite entries from my grandfather reads, "I had to go to the Millers' house to retrieve a pair of mittens, which was stolen by one of the children from another child." If only the television show *Cops* had been around then. Of course there were other, more controversial notes, like "Mr. Davis was drunk and passed out at a bar. I picked him up and drove him home." Does this sound like Mayberry, USA? It was. And that's why *The Andy Griffith Show* is my favorite TV series of all time.

In our community, everybody knew everybody. You know the old saying that it takes a village to raise a child? Well, in many ways, it does. When I got out of line, I was corrected by my mom—and by my neighbors' moms. When I was at my buddy's house, his mom was my mom, too. The paper mill whistle went off three times a day: eight a.m., noon, and five p.m. Saturdays—or any day in the summer—usually began by riding our bikes around the neighborhood and yelling for our pals to join us for a baseball game. If we could round up a dozen or so, we'd ride to the park and play all day long. But we knew that when the noon whistle went off, it was time to sprint home—or to a friend's home—for lunch. Then we'd head right back to the ball field. The evening whistle called us home for dinner.

People weren't worried about kids being kidnapped or hurt. Safety was normal for us. In the winter, hockey replaced baseball. Up until I turned sixteen, I listened for the ten p.m. fire alarm from the village of Carthage, right across the river. That meant curfew had begun. If you were under sixteen, you better head home fast, or the local police would give you a stern lecture.

Many houses had American flags on the front porch on holidays, and most people attended the local parades. Friday night football games and basketball games were always packed. We had "typical" small town cops, a small-town barber (who seemed to somehow cut *everybody's* hair), and plenty of mom-and-pop grocery stores, like Gruner's, right up the street from my house. For a quarter, you could walk out with a Pepsi and a cupcake. If that was too rich, penny candy was still available. We'd sit out front and enjoy our treats. Howard Gruner, the proprietor, was an elderly widower and a very kind man. These stores were real gathering places, not the manufactured ones we see on every corner today.

Several nights a week, I'd walk a mile to the Boys Club to play basketball at night. I don't know why this memory stands out, but I clearly remember walking down sidewalks lined with maple trees and tapping each sap bucket that hung on the trunks. Each one was like a little drum. You could tell how much sap was in the bucket by the sound of the knock.

Even in small towns, I don't see maple syrup buckets hanging from trees anymore. I get sad when I realize that many children will never experience life in a community where neighbors are like family and everyone looks out for one another.

MINDING MY OWN BUSINESS

My siblings and I didn't really receive an allowance. If I wanted money, I had to shovel driveways, but only after our own was shoveled. On snowy mornings, my dad would get us up before school to shovel the driveway so he could go to work. And there were a lot of snow days in West Carthage. I would walk around the neighborhood and shovel driveways for two dollars. I might make around twenty bucks before it was time to go home.

The same went for our lawn mowing "business." As soon as I finished our lawn, I'd fill the mower's tank with gas and push it around the neighborhood, looking for tall grass. When I got a little older, I got a paper route but hated it. I quickly got tired of asking the same people to pay for their subscription, week after week. There were times when a buddy and I would work on a local farm to milk cows or shovel manure—whatever we could do to earn a few bucks. As a teenager, I sometimes went to my cousin's farm on the weekends to help him with his milking. Bobby is not only my cousin but also a lifelong friend. After morning milking, his mom would cook up a breakfast so big I couldn't eat the rest of the day.

I watched my dad in his role as a patrolman and magistrate and found it fascinating. His office was in a front room of our home, and at all hours of the day and night, state troopers and local police would come to our home to have someone arraigned. Those arrested had to be arraigned by the local magistrate prior to being sent to jail, which sometimes included people in handcuffs.

I'd be out mowing the lawn or shoveling the driveway and saw all sorts of colorful characters coming and going. It might seem like a strange or uncomfortable aspect of my childhood, but we were never concerned. In those days there was a tangible respect for law enforcement. I saw it in my father and in the local and state police; they were revered by our community. All the kids in the twin villages respected them greatly, and every adult also knew who our parents were, so there would be no hiding from the truth.

I hope you have similarly fond memories of your formative years, but I realize—all too well—that many people's childhoods were nothing like this. My family and I experienced innocence, peace, security, and everything great about this country. I want *every* American—citizens, legal immigrants, and lawful residents alike—to experience the same thing in their communities. And I know how to help make that a reality for more people.

What I can't figure out is why so many people seem jaded about the future and look on those simpler times with disdain. Our country's innocence has been stolen, but it can be returned.

FOLLOWING THE CALL TO PROTECT AND SERVE

From the time I was in fourth grade, I knew I wanted to be a cop. There was never a moment of doubt. As soon as I graduated high school, I went to Jefferson Community College to study criminal justice, then attended SUNY Polytechnic Institute and earned a bachelor's degree in the subject. As soon as possible, I became a cop in my hometown of West Carthage, New York.

When I first walked into the station wearing my uniform I thought, *Okay, my life starts now.*

I knew it was a small town and that I wouldn't be there forever, but it was the first step and an important step. As corny as it might sound, wearing a badge on my chest and a gun on my hip was almost overwhelming. Yes, I was entrusted with the authority to lock someone up, but I was also there to repay the community that raised me.

My first call on my first night as a police officer was to investigate a report from a babysitter, who was fourteen years old, about a possible intruder. I rushed to the address, parked my patrol car in plain sight, and walked around the house with my flashlight to see if I could see anything. Once I was sure the property was secure, I walked up to the front porch and rang the doorbell. The little girl had a look of such relief on her face when she saw me. I could tell she'd been crying. I settled her down and I told her no one was out there. She then showed me the window someone had attempted to open. I didn't see signs of forced entry, but I believed her. Walking through every room of the house, I checked every window and door to make sure they were all locked.

It was ten thirty p.m., and the parents weren't expected to be home until midnight. There were no cell phones back then, so there was no way to reach them. Thankfully, it was a slow night, and I told the babysitter I'd be in my patrol car, right out in front of the house, until the parents came home. While sitting out there, I saw the living room curtain open and close about every three minutes and realized the babysitter was checking to make sure I was still there.

When the parents finally arrived home, I told them about the events of the evening, and they thanked me over and over. Even though I was well acquainted with the life and work of a cop, this experience made me realize how much the job was really about helping people—scared, vulnerable, good people. Driving the patrol car back to the station for the first time, I knew I had picked the right career.

Sure, I wrote plenty of speeding tickets. Sorry about that, but the speed limits are there for the good of everyone. I had many long nights, changed many flat tires, and intervened in some awkward situations. But when you see how something as simple as your presence can settle the nerves of a frightened family, it's worth it. When you walk around a park during the local field day and a little boy looks up, smiles, and says hello, you remember why you wear the uniform.

Whether dealing with a lost child, a domestic disturbance, or traffic violations, being a police officer is about serving a community. I especially enjoyed helping kids. Occasionally I'd pull over to watch a few minutes of a Little League game and chat with the kids. I was trying to give them the same kind of childhood I had, and the same relationship with law enforcement. Whenever I stopped for a Coke at Gruner's or any of the other local shops, I always talked with kids. I wanted to let them know we were there to help them and to not be afraid of us, ever.

It's not about catching bad guys. It's about protecting the good guys. I suppose you could call it a boring place to be a cop. But, personally, I'd give almost anything to go back to "boring" life in America. And that's what drives me.

BORDERLINE COPS

West Carthage was less than an hour from the Canadian border, and I often went to that area to fish. It seems I have the same effect on fish and criminals—they both seem to scatter when I'm around. But what I lack in talent, I make up for in stubbornness. Anyway, I'd see the occasional Border Patrol agent, but I didn't really know what their job was about.

After about eighteen months in my new role as a police officer, I was on the dock in Alexandria Bay, cleaning some freshly caught fish, and an agent pulled up beside me on his patrol boat. After some friendly fish stories, he learned I was a cop. "We're holding some agent testing, Tom. You should apply." On my way home, I stopped by the local post office and filed an application to take the Border Patrol entrance exam. A few days later I took the test at the Watertown Post Office while being monitored by a couple of Border Patrol agents. There were fewer than ten of us taking the test. Six months later, I received a phone call to schedule an interview.

I wanted to have greater impact in law enforcement, and I had already applied to the New York State Police but hadn't heard back. The Border Patrol hadn't been on my radar, but the chance to go from a local to national level was definitely interesting. And daunting. The application and training process would be tough. I viewed the opportunity with a "can't fail" mindset. Sure, if I didn't make the cut I could have rejoined the police department, but to me it wasn't an option. I couldn't face my family, or my community, if I failed.

When I was twenty-two, my parents drove me and my one suit-case to the Syracuse airport, bound for San Diego, California. This would be only my second time on an airplane. I'd never ventured more than a couple hundred miles from home and was about to land in a completely different world.

THERE'S NO PLACE LIKE HOME

Fast-forward to January 27, 2017—the day I was to retire, almost thirty-three years to the day from when I graduated from the

Border Patrol Academy. In October 2016, I decided to hang it up. It had been a long career, and I was tired. I'd moved around the country at least six times, my family lived in five different homes, and my two boys had attended multiple schools. I was approached by several companies that offered me a generous salary—much more than I ever made with the government. But what really pushed me toward retirement was the previous eight years under the Obama administration, where we really couldn't do the job we had sworn to do. And I was convinced that Hillary Clinton would be our next president. I simply could not handle more of that frustration. When I have a job, I do my absolute best to complete the mission. My passion and drive hadn't faded, but I knew what a Clinton administration would mean.

I announced my retirement in October 2016 in order to give ICE at least ninety days to find a senior leader to transition in. I was the executive associate director for Enforcement and Removal Operations—one of two key leaders, third in command of the agency. In my almost four years in that role, I oversaw the program that removed nearly 1 million illegal aliens from this country. But my colleagues and I could have done even more if we had the support of elected leaders.

When Donald Trump won the presidency, I was amazed and surprised. Mostly, I was happy for the men and women of ICE, because I knew they would be able to do their jobs without ridiculous policies that limited their ability. I thought about canceling my retirement, but I had already committed to a private company and believed that path would be best for me and my family. I served my country for over three decades, and my wife and two sons also sacrificed dearly for this country—many different homes, schools, doctors, and friends—and many missed birthdays, anniversaries, and first days of school. My family also paid the price for my career.

On January 27, 2017, my family and I attended my retirement ceremony. Several hundred people were there, and it was a very emotional day for me. I had lived my dream, a dream I had carried since I was a little boy. I spent a career in law enforcement serving at the highest levels of a federal agency. I felt blessed.

That was also the last day I'd carry a gun and a badge. The next morning I'd wake up and realize I wasn't a cop anymore. I also knew that for the first time in thirty-three years, I would have to stand in line at airport security like everyone else. That was one benefit I'd miss for sure.

After a long and emotional ceremony, I received various gifts, plaques, and tokens of appreciation—including the retirement of my badge, which was given to me along with an exact replica of the weapon I carried for many years. I stood outside in the hallway and shook hands with everyone who stopped by. At one point I was approached by my chief of staff, who said I had an emergency phone call from Department of Homeland Security secretary John Kelly. *Very nice of him to take time to congratulate me,* I thought, as I excused myself and walked to my empty office. All my personal belongings were already stacked in my garage. Secretary Kelly began the call by saying he knew this was bad timing, but he and the president would like me to postpone my retirement and serve as the director of ICE, a two-step promotion.

I confirmed that it was pretty bad timing because I'd just retired. He then informed me that I had not yet officially retired because the paperwork was still on his desk.

Sure, I had heard rumors that I was being considered for the post for weeks, but when the day of my retirement came, I knew they must have been like the many rumors that pass through the halls of government. When the offer was actually made, I was truly caught off guard. I advised Secretary Kelly that I would have to talk to my family, because they had sacrificed so much for so long. Since it was Friday, I asked for the weekend to make the decision. He understood and agreed that my family absolutely needed to be part of this decision, and said he'd call me at eight on Monday morning.

Before we hung up, he asked to say one last thing, and I remember every single word. "Tom, the president of the United States is asking you, a career law enforcement officer, to serve your nation a little bit longer. He needs your help." With that, we ended the call.

I thought about my parents. I thought about what I'd seen on the border and in communities ravaged by needless crime. I thought about the heartbreak of May 13, 2003, in Victoria, Texas. I thought about my hometown of West Carthage. Most of all, I thought about my family. *Is this the right thing to do?*

I've faced down many scary situations in my time, but the thought of telling my wife about the news was truly intimidating. It was a long, slow walk back to the "retirement" party.

FAMILY AND COMMUNITY

My family was against the idea at first, and I was not going to accept the position without their full support. But they also know who I am and why I had chosen to be a law enforcement officer. I may not be the smartest man in the world, but I love the country I was asked to serve. After a long weekend talking with my family, they gave me their support on Sunday night.

As promised, the following Monday I received a call from Secretary Kelly at eight a.m. sharp. I accepted the position of director of ICE. A few hours later the White House called and said the announcement would be made in the early evening. I didn't have to watch the news to know when the press release hit. My phone blew up with calls and messages. At some point I had to turn the phone off so I could get some sleep. The next morning, one of the first calls I received was from my hometown. It was Mark Keddy, owner of one of two bars in West Carthage. I downed my first legal drink there when I turned eighteen. Mark and his family were life-long residents of that village. He knew my family, knew me before I became a cop, and knew all about my ambitions.

When I was home from college my friends and I often met at Keddy's, and there were a few times I found myself in no condition to drive. I would let Mark know I was leaving Dad's car there and walk the mile home. Trudging through knee-high snow at two a.m. was never fun, but I'm thankful I had the sense to make the right decision. The following morning my dad yelled upstairs, "Tom! I see the car keys, but where's the car?!"

I'd yell back that I left it at Keddy's because I drank a little too much. But what I remember most is that my dad never got upset or yelled at me about the situation. He'd put on his coat, grab the keys, and walk the mile to Keddy's. Being a local judge, and being my dad, he knew what I was doing. I was protecting my dreams of a career in law enforcement. I know Mark and his dad, Clarence, probably had a few laughs at my dad's expense when he showed up at the bar the next morning. But my dad took it in stride. I was raised in a village, and that village took care of me.

The first morning I showed up at the ICE headquarters building as the new director, I was met with many handshakes and smiles. I had to explain many times that the retirement function a few days ago was not a joke and that I had had no idea I was coming back. I told the story of the John Kelly phone call a hundred times that day.

The first people who came to my office were a group of attorneys from the Ethics Department. Since I was now the ICE director, and since everyone in the building now worked for me, I had to return every retirement gift I'd received a few days earlier. The second person to visit my office was the assistant director of the ICE office of public affairs, Barbara Gonzalez. She started listing all the media outlets requesting interviews. "We have to figure out what we're going to do about the press, Mr. Homan. Here are the requests for interviews, from the *Washington Post*, *New York Times*, CBS, NBC, ABC, FOX News, and a hundred more!"

"Okay." I sighed. "Let's make a list of who you think we should respond to first, and put them in order. Number one is WWNY-TV."

She wrote it down, then looked at me, puzzled. "Sir, I'm not familiar with them."

"It's my hometown station in Watertown, New York," I replied, trying to hide a grin.

"With all due respect, you have Fox News, CNN, and every national news network asking for interviews."

"I am who I am because of my hometown. They raised me, and they are going to have the first interview."

A few minutes later, I received a call from my old area code, so I answered. "Tom, you don't know me, but I'm Jeff Cole. You knew my uncle."

"Yeah, he was wrestling coach!"

"Well, Dick is my uncle. I'm a reporter for WWNY, and would like to have an interview with you."

"You're not going to believe it, Jeff, but I just told my assistant to set this appointment up. We'll make it happen as soon as I can fly up there. By the way, how did you get my number?"

"Mark Keddy gave it to me." That was thanks to the inner workings of a small town.

I caught the next flight to Syracuse and had my first television interview as acting ICE director with my local station. This was my way of thanking my friends and neighbors for all the success I've enjoyed in my career. The community put me first, and for once in my life I wanted to put them first. West Carthage made me who I am. I'll never forget what I learned from the farmers and factory workers there, who work very hard for very little money. I wanted them to be proud of me and to know I was proud of them.

That week, I received hundreds of phone calls of congratulations from extended family, former coworkers, and friends I hadn't talked to in thirty years. I still don't know how so many people had my cell phone number, but that's life in a small town. And that's why I fight.

BORDERS, IMMIGRATION, AND YOUR COMMUNITY

Immigration is the most controversial and emotional issue this country faces. In 2016, a president was elected on this issue. I am not a politician; I am a career law enforcement officer who has seen too much preventable suffering during my career. From the front lines as a border patrol agent to serving as a special agent investigating criminal organizations that smuggle and traffic in women and children, I've overseen the national operation of arresting, detaining, and removing criminal aliens in the interior of the United States. I have personally carried out every task I've asked the men and women of ICE to do every day. I was the first ICE director who came up through every rung on the ladder.

It's time to share what illegal immigration and a porous border actually mean to the people of our country. It's not a partisan issue, and the solutions are not complex. Now is the time to separate fact from fiction and fix this issue that has claimed too many victims and divided this nation.

Illegal immigration is not a victimless crime. I fight for the victims so that others will never experience the violence I've witnessed. If you've seen what I've seen, you'd be passionate about fixing the problem, too.

WHAT KIND OF COMMUNITY DO YOU WANT?

The crisis on the border is not controversial. Everyone with two eyes and a shred of honesty can see through the excuses aand distractions. We all know there's an enormous problem. In the following pages, I'll present a true assessment of the situation—the real story on the ground, and what most media won't report.

We'll explore—without the usual BS—the issues of human trafficking, cartels, border walls, racism, "zero tolerance" policies, and sanctuary cities. I'll also present simple, commonsense solutions for illegal immigration and border security.

I'm not afraid to deal with every issue, every accusation, and every lie head-on—and you shouldn't be afraid, either. When you know the facts and the true story on the border, you'll be ready to join me in defense of our country.

This is no longer just a border issue. Illegal immigration affects every town and city in this nation. This matters to your local community and to the community we call America. Enforcing the law and fixing our problems are all about creating an environment for neighborhoods, cities, and states to thrive—and protecting our way of life for citizens and for those who would become citizens.

TWO

IMMIGRATION AND THE LAW

*145,262 convicted criminals were removed by ICE in 2018,
and 4,818 gang members were arrested.*
—HOMELAND SECURITY INVESTIGATIONS

West Carthage, New York, was basically all I knew of the world as a twenty-two-year-old. Even the college and university I attended were less than a two-hour drive from home. Flying to California—a place I'd only seen in the movies—made me both excited and nervous. Remember, this was 1984, and the internet, social media, and cell phones as we know them today weren't yet around.

In October 1984, after a long flight to San Diego to begin my job as a border patrol agent, my one suitcase and I took a taxi to San Ysidro, where Border Patrol headquarters were located. There was a Motel 6 a few blocks away, so I booked a room. As soon as I checked into the motel, I walked to HQ, admiring the palm trees as the sun set. *It's only a ten-minute walk,* I calculated. *So I need to leave by 7:40 in the morning to make sure I'm on time for my eight a.m. appointment.* As I headed back for the day, I picked up some Kentucky Fried Chicken and celebrated my journey with a feast in my motel room. I'd never had KFC before, and it lived up to the hype.

Just as I finished the last drumstick, a huge commotion erupted outside. As I watched from the balcony, a helicopter flew overhead with spotlights glaring. On the street below, several law enforcement vehicles and three-wheelers were chasing a group of young men. I had a front row seat to the action! In just a few minutes the group was surrounded and captured, while the helicopter kept the area lit up. In the bright light I could see the pursuers were all border patrol agents and could only assume the group of men were illegal aliens.

I wasn't in Mayberry, USA, anymore. I'd never seen anything like that before, and I wondered, *What the hell did I get myself into?*

LINE UP AND SHUT UP

The next morning I woke up early and arrived at the Border Patrol sector office as planned. A group started to form in the parking lot of the main building, and everyone introduced themselves. It was quickly apparent that we were all new trainees. We compared rumors and stories about what we heard about the academy and the job. One thing was certain: We were all a bit nervous. We were told to line up and shut up. After a brief and impolite welcome we were escorted into a barracks building and seated in a classroom. The two senior agents introduced themselves as our caretakers for the next three days, to prepare us for the academy in Georgia.

For the next two days we filled out endless paperwork, stood in straight lines at attention, said "Yes, sir" a lot, and tried to absorb all the new information—including the fact that our meager compensation package didn't include any retirement benefits. "We're trying to figure something out, and will keep you posted. For now, we're putting 7.5 percent of your paycheck into an account," they told us.

The infamous twenty-year federal retirement that we all counted on was gone. That was unwelcome news, but as far as I was concerned there was no turning back. Those of us who made it through the academy would earn an annual salary of eighteen thousand dollars. We weren't joining the border patrol for the perks.

On the third and final day of orientation, they drove us downtown to a San Diego uniform shop that promised to measure us and make our rough duty and Class A uniforms the same day, "while you wait." They were right about the waiting part. Thirty of us walked out of there with five sets of uniforms each.

The next day, I flew to Jacksonville, Florida, with the other recruits and my two suitcases, one with my personal belongings I had brought from home and the other stuffed with fresh uniforms and gear. Our "caretakers" took us to the airport and handed us our tickets. For the first time, they treated us like a part of the family and wished us good luck. While we waited for our plane, they gave us hints on how to succeed at the academy. It was well known that the Border Patrol Academy was probably the toughest academy in federal law enforcement because, in addition to learning the various laws, high-speed pursuit, firearms, and self-defense, we were required to read, speak, and understand the Spanish language. The rate of successful graduates ranged around 60 percent, which meant four out of ten wouldn't graduate.

For someone like me, from a small town in upstate New York who had never even heard the Spanish language used, I was in for a long, difficult experience. I didn't know the difference between *buenas noches* and *burrito*. One of the caretaker border patrol agents in San Diego told me to get a Walkman as soon as I arrived to the academy. If you're under the age of thirty, you probably don't even know what a Walkman or cassette tape is. Anyway, he told me to go to the Spanish Lab at the academy and check out Spanish conversation tapes and listen to them as often as I had the chance—between classes, at night while in bed, on the weekends—because I needed to develop an "ear" for the language and get used to the speed and the dialects.

I bought a Walkman at the airport before boarding the plane. I was determined not to fail, and I'd do everything I could to succeed.

When we landed at the Jacksonville airport, Border Patrol vans picked us up and transported us one hour north to the Federal Law Enforcement Training Center in Glynco, Georgia. At the time, every federal law enforcement agency except the FBI trained there. Our vans were met by Border Patrol instructors in dress uniform. They gave us our dorm assignments and told us to bed down and show up in uniform at 0700 the following morning in the very same parking lot. "Don't be late, don't show up unshaven, have all your brass polished, shoes shined, uniform neatly pressed with a straight gig line, or there will be hell to pay!"

There was an inspection every morning before training, and we had to march in formation from class to class. No other agency operated that way on campus. The Border Patrol had, and still has, a high esprit de corps. That morale developed pride in each of us as we wore the uniform. Every other agency would watch us march to class every day, and I'm sure others mocked us, but it was part of a team-building exercise. I was in decent physical shape when I arrived at the academy, but with all the running and physical drills, I dropped twenty-five pounds. The law classes were not difficult, thanks to my college training, so I spent most of my time studying Spanish. I went through a case of batteries listening to that Walkman. After about twelve weeks I could conduct an interview or interrogation in Spanish and understand the responses. Reading the Miranda warning was a must, and I can still recite it in Spanish to this day.

Around Christmas, I befriended a Texan named Robert. My parents had a winter home in Florida, about a two-hour drive from the academy, so we drove down to see them one weekend. Robert was from Vanhorn, Texas, and spoke Spanish very well, even though he's a gringo. As we got into the car, he announced, "All right, Homan. We're leaving the base and won't speak English on the drive to and from your folks' place. If you don't understand something, ask me to repeat it slowly—in Spanish."

On the way back from the visit, we were driving north on I-95 and just about ready to hit the Georgia line. Robert was driving and we both had our Walkman headphones on. I was listening to Spanish tapes, which was much easier than using my limited skills to converse with him. We spotted a Florida highway patrolman observing passing traffic, and as we went past I made eye contact with him and knew we were about to be pulled over. I took my earplugs out and told Robert to take his out because I thought it might be illegal to have them on while driving. Sure enough, he pulled us over.

The officer asked Robert if he was listening to the Walkman and he said yes. I explained that we were Border Patrol recruits, had an exam the next day, and were listening to Spanish tapes. The trooper asked to see Robert's Walkman, and I was surprised it was still on. What I didn't realize at the time was that, after I shut my Walkman off, I also shut Robert's off but I pushed the switch too far—past the Off position and into Radio mode. When the trooper put the device up to his ear, he was greeted with the sounds of Madonna singing "Like a Virgin."

Long story short, Robert got a traffic citation, and I spent the next two hours apologizing. In Spanish, of course.

The academy had a Spanish quiz every week, and each started with the same words: *"Escuchan solamente, no escriben nada,"* which means "Listen only, don't write anything down." The instructor played a tape of someone telling a story in Spanish. After the story finished, the recording repeated one sentence at a time, and we had to write down the exact English translation. This was an exercise we'd do many times while at the academy and pretty much daily in our career.

Every Monday morning, as we stood at attention at seven a.m., there were fewer and fewer classmates standing beside me. I was scared to death of disappointing my family and my village. I didn't want to go home with my tail between my legs. I worked tirelessly to succeed, and the effort paid off. I graduated with grades above 90 percent, including a 93 in Spanish. I refused to quit, was afraid of failure, and never worked so hard in my life.

When I stood on the graduation stage, wearing that gold tin badge, I again knew my dreams were becoming real. I wanted my life and career to have the greatest impact, and this was the next level.

Even though graduation was one of the greatest days in my life, it was also sad. The men and women I trained with for the past five months would soon be deployed to their home stations around the country. We truly had become a family. Those few months at the academy instilled a sense of camaraderie that stayed with us forever. Once you wear the green, you will always bleed green.

¿HABLAS ESPAÑOL?

After graduation, I drove up to West Carthage with my parents and was home for a few days until I headed back to the airport. I'd be stationed in Campo, California.

After landing in San Diego, I asked the taxi driver to take me to an area where there were used car lots. With suitcases in tow, I walked around several lots until I found the car I wanted—and could afford. I had saved almost five months' worth of paychecks, since I'd had no expenses at the academy. My silver 1980 Ford Mustang and I cruised to the nearest 7-Eleven store and grabbed an apartment-finder book. I stayed in a motel the first night, and the next day I drove up to the Campo Station, which was about an hour from San Diego. The first person I met was a supervisor named Gary. He seemed like a great guy, and I could tell he was a seasoned veteran, with his white hair, white mustache, and well-worn uniform. His gun hung low from years of wear. I told him I was looking for an apartment, and he said there were some historic apartments right across the street from the station. They were old army barracks from the 1940s and home to the Buffalo Soldiers.

During World War II, the apartment building had been an active military base known as Camp Lockett, and the Army had a cavalry unit there, which patrolled the border on horseback. The old barracks were renovated into makeshift apartments. I moved into the barracks the next day. I didn't have any furniture, but the tiny apartment had a refrigerator, a stove, and a shower—everything a young agent needed. The best part of renting in the barracks was being back in a small community. The population of Campo was around two thousand people, the same as my hometown, which brought an immediate sense of comfort.

On my first day at work I was again greeted by Gary and went on patrol with him. He gave me lots of priceless advice, including how to interact with people on the border. "Look, Tom, you still have months of post-academy training and probation. You're a lot like me. You grew up in a place where you never heard the Spanish language before. When you arrest an alien, talk to him a lot—not only at processing, but when he's in the car. Ask about his family. Ask about where he grew up, and what his childhood was like. Use every opportunity to hear and speak the language."

I took his advice to heart.

From my first days as a Border Patrol agent, I went the extra mile to communicate with every Spanish-speaking person I encountered. I still do. When I detained someone, before taking them to the border or the local facility for processing, I'd ask if they were hungry or thirsty and share my lunch with them. In Spanish I'd ask, "Do you mind sitting and talking with me while we eat?" I never had anyone refuse. In fact, the vast majority of these encounters were respectful, even though the circumstances were tough.

Sometimes I'd invite them to correct my pronunciation or choice of words. I wanted to become fluent in their native language, to improve communication, to show respect. Most of the feedback I received was something like "You sound too professional, like you're talking down to us. You need to learn more slang, because people will open up to you more."

"How would you say this phrase?" I'd ask, and my real Spanish classes began. Communication 101, really.

We had a Coke machine in the processing area—the proceeds went to our recreation fund. I'd often buy a couple cans and have a man-to-man conversation, outside of the law enforcement context. "Why did you come to the United States? What kind of work do you do? What village did you grow up in?" This was, and is, the way all my fellow agents operate, whenever possible. I tell you this because you probably won't see a news story about how agents really interact, every single day—when they wear the badge, and when they don't.

Just the other day, my neighbor had some yard work done. The crew's truck was blocking my driveway. So I walked up to them and said, "Excuse me sir, can you move your truck?" I could tell he didn't speak English, and neither did his crew. Some people would assume that my first inclination would be to ask them for their identification. I feel the need to point out the fact that this is never the case. Unlike many on the Left, I don't see the world through the lens of citizenship, race, or language. Anyway, I then asked him in Spanish. With a surprised smile, he nodded and moved the truck.

One of my favorite restaurants is owned by a family from El Salvador, who immigrated here many years ago and became citizens. As far as my vocabulary takes me, I try to only speak Spanish while at the restaurant. Their family gets a kick out of it because they say I have a "funny accent." And I still get a kick out of it because knowing another language opens up the world in a wonderful way.

YOU'RE A HYPOCRITE, TOM

I know what some might be thinking. *Okay, Homan. If you care about people so much, how could you arrest them for simply crossing a border?*

My answer is that in this country, the law is more important than my emotions or the feelings of any politician. But in addition, the law, applied equally, is one of the things that makes the United States a place where people want to live. I am not, and have never been, anti-immigrant. I am anti–*illegal* immigration. There's a night and day difference. I can't blame anyone who wants to be a part of the greatest country on earth, but no one should disrespect our laws. Our laws, equal justice under the law, and respect for the law are what make this country great.

We take so much for granted in the United States. Many of the people trying to immigrate here come from countries with corrupt governments—from the president to the local police. Turning our country into a place where laws are not respected does not help anyone—whether they are citizens or immigrants.

Leftists don't want "equal justice under the law." They want an ever-expanding list of policies and rules that create confusion, handcuff law enforcement, and increase human suffering.

The law is impersonal, for good reason. The solution to our border crisis is not to ignore certain laws that some people feel are not nice. More than ever, we must reaffirm the fact that law and order are essential to our way of life. We must hold our lawmakers accountable to follow the law and create legislation to address the challenges we face. We need laws that create transparency, stability, and peace.

I have a few suggestions. Stay tuned.

LAWLESSNESS, LIES, AND SOME FACTS

In recent months there have been an alarming number of baseless and absurd claims by some far-Left Democrats that compare US Immigration and Customs Enforcement detention facilities for illegal aliens to the Nazi concentration camps, where millions of Jews and others were tortured and brutally murdered. The comparison is irrational and dishonors the memory of all the men, women, and children killed by the Nazis. It also dishonors the memories of all the members of the US military who bravely fought in World War II to defeat the Nazis. And the comparison falsely implies that hardworking ICE officers dedicated to enforcing US immigration laws are in the same category as Nazi mass murderers—an outrageous and delusional lie.

The ridiculous comparison is an attempt to push a false narrative that they hope will convince the American people that no one entering the United States illegally should be detained.

A United States without detention capability will only worsen our immigration crisis. If we do not have the ability to detain those who illegally enter our country until they see a judge and plead their case, we will never solve the issue of unlawful border crossings, and they will skyrocket beyond the already unprecedented levels.

Amazingly, we have several Democrats (including self-proclaimed socialists) running for their party's presidential nomination who have pledged to end immigration detention and what they call "for-profit prisons." These candidates—so-called lawmakers—willfully ignore reality. If we lose the ability to detain those who intentionally enter our country illegally, especially single adults, we lose the border.

Here are a few facts that the Left does not want you to know.

Some 72 percent of all migrants detained in an ICE facility are congressionally mandated to be detained. In other words, laws passed by Congress and signed by past presidents require that ICE detain these people. If ICE released them, the agency would be breaking the law.

Nearly 90 percent of migrants arrested by ICE in the interior of the United States are either convicted criminals or face pending criminal charges. If you simply look at the current recidivism rates, about half of criminals will re-offend within a year, and as many as 75 percent will re-offend within five years. Despite the complaints of many liberals, the fact is that these "prisons" make our communities safer.

ICE contracts most of its detention to outside companies that construct and operate detention facilities—not only for the federal government, but also for state and local governments. These companies are used because they maintain detention facilities at a higher quality and lower cost than the government can provide. When I was the ICE director, I can tell you that some of our most expensive detainee beds were in facilities that ICE owned. Using outside contractors that run facilities like this as their core business function saves millions of dollars in taxpayer funds and increases the quality of care those being detained receive.

The quality of care afforded those in ICE-contracted detention facilities is better than you will find in any federal or state institution. ICE also contracts some short-term beds from local sheriffs. When I was the ICE director, numerous sheriffs across the country would end their contract with ICE or refuse to contract with ICE to hold our detainees because our detention standards were too high. Numerous sheriffs told me that they would not provide such high standards for illegal aliens in their jails, because they don't provide these programs to jailed US citizens.

ICE is fully committed to the highest level of quality, providing safe, secure, and humane environments for those in ICE custody and care. Contracted facilities operate pursuant to and in compliance with strict governmental standards as well as accreditation and certification standards set by medical accreditation agencies, educational agencies and the ICE detention standards. ICE detention facilities are managed based on the standards set by applicable third-party accreditation agencies, including the American Correctional Association, the National Commission on Correctional Healthcare, the Commission on Jail Standards, and the Joint Commission on Health Care.

The standards within which ICE facilities operate were crafted to improve medical and mental health services, increase access to legal services and religious expression, improve communication with detainees with limited English proficiency, improve the process for reporting and responding to complaints, reinforce protections against sexual abuse and assault, and increase recreation and visitation.

Here's the bottom line: No one wants to be held in detention. No one would argue that being held is a pleasant experience. And right now a huge influx of illegal aliens is straining the capacity of ICE to detain them. But federal officials are doing their utmost to hold detainees in facilities that meet high standards and to keep the detainees healthy. To compare federal detention facilities to Nazi concentration camps is hateful propaganda that no one should believe.

Unless more citizens speak up, those lies will spread. I will not be silenced. But we need your voice, too.

LAWLESS LAWMAKERS

In 2019, ICE prepared to conduct one of their nationwide operations to arrest and deport aliens who were previously ordered by a judge to leave the country. Democrat leaders, including Nancy Pelosi, held a press conference to instruct those who have violated our nation's laws on how they can evade federal law enforcement. Speaker Pelosi read the following statement: "An ICE deportation warrant is not the same as a search warrant. If that is the only document ICE brings to a home raid, agents do not have the legal right to enter a home. If ICE agents don't have a warrant signed by a judge, a person may refuse to open the door and let them in."

The Speaker of the House, a "lawmaker" for decades, actually instructed people to evade the laws that Congress enacted. What other laws can we ignore? What other law enforcement officers should we evade? Can I ignore the tax law and not pay my taxes? The Speaker seems to believe we can pick and choose what laws we want to abide by, and which laws we can ignore. This behavior by Democrat politicians—on Capitol Hill and in our cities —will result in many more unintended consequences.

Lawlessness puts the public in more danger, and it certainly puts Border Patrol Agents and ICE officers in more danger. Disrespect for the law will lead to unrest, violence, and death—it always has and always will.

In the summer of 2019, an armed man, who had attended a protest at an ICE contract facility in Washington state, tried to burn down the building where American civilians and hundreds of illegal aliens from Mexico, Guatemala, El Salvador, Honduras, and many other countries were detained. This man lost his life when police were forced to shoot him. This is just one aspect of what happens when politicians spread lies about their fellow citizens in law enforcement and incite hatred.

These ICE facilities have doctors, nurses, dentists, and psychologists to treat detainees; recreation areas; law libraries; and clean beds. They provide three nutritious meals a day. Do you think the person who attempted to burn that facility down and kill hundreds of people ever heard any of these facts? Not if he was listening to the Democrats, who want to abolish ICE and all detention facilities.

Who pays the price for all these lies? You, me, and our neighbors—who will be less safe if ICE isn't allowed to do its job and arrest, detain, and remove those who the law says must be removed.

AMERICA BY THE BOOK

Maybe we can agree that without laws, and enforcement of those laws, we don't have a country—a country we want to live in, anyway, and certainly not the United States of America we know and love. Without borders, we are not a country. No country in the world has open borders. We have the right to defend our sovereignty.

In July 2019, Representative Rashida Tlaib had this to say about ICE: "It is a broken system. It needs to be audited—it needs to be completely dismantled. We didn't have ICE years ago—before 9/11—and I can tell you we were fine."

We were fine? Really?

ICE was formed, in part, because of the tragedy of September 11, 2001. Some of the terrorists were here illegally.

Around the time of Representative Tlaib's comments, I testified in Congress, looked her in the eye, and told her, "If you don't like what ICE does, change the law, and ICE will enforce whatever laws you enact."

She nodded in approval and promised to work on solutions.

Just kidding. Of course she didn't.

ICE and every federal law enforcement agency enforce the laws our representatives enact. If they don't like the laws, they should stand up and legislate instead of putting our brave men and women in danger. Do your job. But don't you dare vilify the men and women that leave the safety of their homes every day to defend this nation.

And speaking of Nazis, I'd like to inform our esteemed lawmakers that ICE has removed hundreds of actual Nazis from the United States over the years and sent them back to face trial. As recently as 2018, ICE deported the last known Nazi collaborator living in the US, a former Polish labor camp guard named Jakiw Palij, who resided for many years in Queens, New York. I don't remember any congresspeople objecting to that deportation.

CALIFORNIA NIGHTMARE

The Democrat-controlled California legislature is determined to stop the Trump administration from enforcing our current immigration laws. By doing this, the legislature makes the absurd claim that it has the power to ignore federal law. Their latest effort would eventually ban the Immigration and Customs Enforcement agency from housing illegal aliens in privately operated prisons in California.

Such a ban is a dangerous move that wouldn't succeed in stopping the detention of illegal aliens. It would simply raise detention costs for US taxpayers and result in illegal aliens being held under less-favorable conditions. So instead of helping illegal aliens—as California Democrats claim they want to do—their legislation would actually hurt the migrants.

Governor Gavin Newsom signed a bill in October 2019 that prohibits immigrant detention facilities and private prisons from operating in California. Assembly Bill 32 prevents the state, beginning in 2020, from entering into or renewing contracts with these companies—and phases out such facilities by 2028. To show you how blatantly partisan this is, the California legislature never took action to stop the detention of illegal aliens in private prisons when President Barack Obama was in office. Yet under the Obama administration, ICE was detaining illegal aliens in private prisons in exactly the same manner as is occurring today under the Trump administration.

In fact, in 2012 alone, ICE arrested and removed a record 409,000 illegal aliens from the US. And the Obama administration approved adding three thousand family detention beds and the so-called cages to hold detainees. Yet Democrats didn't try to stop the Obama administration's enforcement of our immigration laws. That's because the Democrats aren't really concerned with protecting illegal aliens. Their real focus is scoring political points as the Democrat Party moves even farther left.

If I was still the ICE director and California shut down the detention of illegal aliens in private prisons, I would be forced to immediately move all detainees out of the state and detain them elsewhere. Unfortunately, this would move them away from their families and community support. It would also move them away from a structured immigration advocacy and immigration attorney network.

The illegal aliens will most likely be housed in county jails in other states that have much lower detention standards than

ICE detention facilities, which are already over capacity. And it's important to note that there are no ICE family detention facilities in California, so no children are being held there. A number of statistics prove detainees are much better off in the ICE facilities the California legislature voted to close. But let's look at just one statistic: the number of deaths of people in custody.

All detention facilities want to hold deaths to the lowest possible number, of course. But according to the Justice Department, in state prisons there is an average death rate of 256 out of every 100,000 inmates. The death rate in federal prisons is 225 out of 100,000 inmates. But at ICE detention facilities, the death rate is less than three out of each 100,000 inmates—dramatically lower than comparable jails and prisons. Moving illegal aliens out of ICE facilities to local jails doesn't do them any favors; it places them in worse conditions.

In addition, almost 90 percent of illegal aliens arrested by ICE in the interior of the US are either convicted criminals or being held on pending criminal charges that go beyond violating immigration laws. The bill passed by the California legislature also bars the US Marshals Service from detaining prisoners in privately run detention facilities in California. The people arrested by the Marshals Service include some of the worst criminals and public safety threats in the world. If ICE and the Marshals Service simply violated federal law and released all the people they are holding in California, you can be sure that tragedy would follow, as innocent Californians became victims of crime. Despite the Democrats' attempts to make our immigration laws meaningless, ICE is not going to stop carrying out its congressionally mandated duty to follow the law.

For the benefit of Democrat politicians, let me recap what we were all taught in elementary school. Congress and the president enact federal laws. Federal agencies, state legislatures, and individuals do not. I assure you that if Congress and the president enacted new immigration laws, ICE officers would follow those laws. But blaming police officers for giving you a speeding ticket, complaining about the Internal Revenue Service for collecting your taxes, or demonizing ICE officers for enforcing immigration laws makes no sense.

Open borders advocates are free to run for the House, for Senate, or for president and work to change the law themselves. But until the law changes, federal law enforcement agencies have to enforce the law.

THE SOLUTION IS UP TO US

In the chapters that follow, I'll reveal what's really happening on the border, and within our dysfunctional immigration system. I'll also address every contentious immigration issue dividing our country, present indisputable facts, and do my best to bring reasonable Americans together around solutions. By the way, "reasonable" means that I'm not counting on many in Congress to do what's right. It's up to us.

THREE

THE REAL STORY ON OUR SOUTHERN BORDER

981,586 pounds of narcotics and $56,000,000 in cash were seized at the Southern border in 2018.
—DEPARTMENT OF HOMELAND SECURITY

In Fiscal Year 2019, the Border Patrol took 851,000 people into custody, the most apprehensions in twelve years.
—US BORDER PATROL

Two numbers stand out from my first Border Patrol assignment, in Campo, California: thirty-five and fifty-three. The station had thirty-five agents. When you divide that up among three shifts and factor days off, the usual manpower on shift was about eight agents. We were responsible for approximately fifty-three miles of border. If situations got hairy, your backup could be twenty minutes away—or more.

Backup not only meant other Border Patrol agents; there were resident San Diego County sheriff's deputies and resident California highway patrolmen in the area. The term *resident* referred to the fact that they lived in the general area and often worked out of their homes in order to minimize response times. I still remember the three sheriffs and two highway patrolmen who lived and worked near Campo. If anything happened after ten p.m. on a given night, they could be called out. Even so, response time in the days before GPS and smartphones was sketchy at best. Bottom line, in such a remote area every law enforcement officer counted on each other. The color of the uniform or the words on a shoulder patch didn't matter. We had each other's backs, and we all took comfort in that fact. It was truly the Wild West.

The dangers for any Border Patrol agent were obvious, but we were also the designated backup for the sheriffs and highway patrol. There were times when I "became" a police officer, for instance, when we were asked by the sheriff to respond to the only bar in Campo, the Old Oak Inn—or a nearby bar called the Dogpatch, which was a favorite haunt of bikers. If a fight broke out and law enforcement was called, the Border Patrol was often first on the scene to try to keep the peace until the deputies arrived. We had a 24/7 law enforcement presence, and we were usually closer than the highway patrol. By the time the sheriff arrived, we usually had tempers under control, a few drunks in handcuffs, and some minor injuries as a result of bikers fighting us. I was lucky: I never lost a fight.

A few months into my new job, I left the station around six p.m. and headed to a friend's house for dinner. I still had my uniform on and was driving my old, beat-up silver 1980 Mustang. About a mile past the station I came across a California Highway Patrol officer who had pulled over four rough-looking bikers just down the road from the Dogpatch. I drove by slowly and flashed him the "four sign," waving four fingers out the window (code 4 means, "Is everything okay?"). The officer quickly gave me the "no" sign.

I immediately pulled over and walked up beside him. He had called for a tow truck to remove two of the choppers, which were not registered or insured. After he advised the bikers about the tow truck, they informed him they'd be long gone by the time the truck arrived. And one of the bikers added that the officer would be "laying in the middle of the road with his ass kicked." As soon as they had made the threat, I pulled up on the situation. Needless to say, I waited until both bikes were loaded up and one biker was arrested for terroristic threats against a law enforcement officer. I was late for dinner that night, but the officer and I were safe.

I can't tell you how many other times I waved "four" at the highway patrol or sheriff and the response was always, "Okay." This was the first time an officer didn't wave me off and needed immediate help. However, in the four years that I served in Campo, I received many more alerts to help. All men and women in uniform are brave and face real danger every day, and it's always comforting to see another uniform arrive when things get dangerous. The camaraderie in law enforcement is strong. Even if we had personal differences with one another, in a time of need we were all one.

THE FRONT LINE OF OUR CRISIS

As Border Patrol agents, we stood on the front line, arresting illegal aliens—which sometimes involved fights, car chases, and even a shooting. I know what it's like to stand in the bushes in the pitch darkness at two o'clock in the morning, waiting for the group of aliens who had just set off a sensor on the trail. I didn't know how many would approach, or if they were Mexican citizens looking for a better life or heavily armed drug mules. Because flashlights can be seen from a great distance, I had to hide in total darkness until they were within about one hundred feet. As if I wasn't already on high alert, the sound of rattlesnakes took the experience to another level.

But that was nothing compared to what I'd soon witness in the California desert. On our patrols, agents would regularly find dead bodies on remote trails. These bodies were not in a casket at a funeral home; they lay dead and decomposing on the dirt. Many were left to die by criminal alien smugglers, because they were sick, unable to walk, and no longer a commodity that could bring cash to their organization. Nothing prepares you for the sight of your first corpse, in the middle of nowhere, covered with bugs or partially eaten by coyotes. The sight and the smell took me to a place in my heart I had never been.

Early in my career I came across what looked like a drunk illegal alien, wandering along a dirt road just north of the border near Tecate. I carefully approached him in my Ram Charger pickup and noticed he was carrying a large stick in his right hand. As I got within a few yards, it was clear that this stick was actually a bone—a femur from a human being. After much time and effort, he was able to lead us to the location of some other bones, which had been ravaged by coyotes. After a quick call to dispatch, several sheriff's deputies showed up and took over the investigation. I continued my patrol along that dirt road, shook my head, and thought, *Welcome to the Border Patrol, Homan.*

Certain politicians and media personalities routinely bash our Border Patrol Agents. But how many of them would put a gun on their hip, a Kevlar vest around their chest, and stand in the desert to take on whoever came down that trail, knowing the nearest law enforcement could be thirty minutes away? Probably none, but that doesn't stop them from vilifying the brave men and women who patrol our borders so citizens can sleep safely at night.

REALITY VERSUS POLITICAL THEATER

I've had the honor of being asked to testify before Congress many times. First, in a hearing conducted shortly after the murderous incident in Victoria, Texas, and most recently as a private citizen and taxpayer—like you—free to speak without fear of pissing off bosses or violating the Hatch Act. They can't fire me; they work for me! If you've seen any of my appearances, you know I walked into a political theater but refused to use their script, because it's not about me. Frankly, there are many places I'd rather be than in a committee hearing talking to folks who don't support the men and women of the Border Patrol or ICE—and have no idea what it's really like on our southern border.

On July 12, 2019, I testified before the Committee on Oversight and Reform. In the hope that my perspective on the border crisis would be taken seriously, I told the members a little about my lifetime of service. Here's a recap, in the hope that it will embolden you to join me in the fight.

I started my career in 1984 as a Border Patrol agent at the Campo Station within the San Diego Border Patrol sector. During that time I arrested many illegal aliens and seized many narcotics that were smuggled into the US. After serving several years as a frontline border patrol agent, I became a special agent with US Immigration and Naturalization Service. As a special agent with INS, I was tasked with the criminal investigation into alien smuggling, human trafficking, immigration fraud, and worksite enforcement. I climbed the ranks within the INS to the assistant district director of investigations in both San Antonio and Dallas, Texas. In this role I was in charge of all special agents and criminal investigations, which included hundreds of counties and several states.

In 2003, upon the creation of DHS, I became an assistant special agent in charge (ASAC). In this position I oversaw several ICE offices and numerous investigations into immigration crime, narcotics trafficking, gun trafficking, human trafficking, child predator crimes, and various other customs-related offenses. As an ASAC with ICE Homeland Security Investigations (HSI), I oversaw the enforcement of over four hundred criminal statutes. In 2009, I was promoted to assistant director of enforcement at ICE headquarters, where I oversaw all interior immigration enforcement operations within the United States. I was later promoted to deputy executive associate director and then the executive associate director (EAD) of ICE Enforcement and Removal Operations. As the EAD I oversaw all interior enforcement operations, including arrests, detention, and removal of those illegally in the US and ordered removed by an immigration judge. In my three and a half years as the EAD of this division, I oversaw the removal of approximately 1 million illegal aliens.

I retired on January 27, 2017—and you already know how that retirement party went. I then served as the acting director of ICE for eighteen months, until my second retirement on June 30, 2018.

Yes, there's a border crisis. Even my former colleague, Jeh Johnson, the former Homeland Security secretary under President Obama, agreed, calling the situation on the US-Mexico border "very definitely a crisis" in 2019. What is happening on our southern border is unprecedented in several ways. Seventy percent of those entering illegally are either family units or unaccompanied children. It's also unprecedented that a majority of those crossing are abusing our asylum laws and making fraudulent claims to exploit the loopholes that Congress has refused to close. Add to this the vilification of the American patriots who serve as Border Patrol agents, ICE officers, and ICE agents, and you can see a perfect storm is building.

I don't blame average citizens of either political party, and I don't even fully blame illegal aliens looking for a better life. The root of the problem is the unwillingness of Congress to address the loopholes that are causing this crisis—and incentivizing criminal activity at the border. I spent my year and a half as the ICE director talking about solutions, and I have continued speaking out ever since. The calls for action have fallen on deaf ears because, for some unfathomable reason, there is more interest in open borders and resisting our president. Securing our border should not be a partisan issue. Whether you are a Republican or Democrat, you should want to know who goes in and out of our country.

POWER, MONEY, AND VOTES

From my experience, the only reason an elected official would be against a tightly secured border is because of a personal quest for power. It's the same reason Leftist Democrats are opposed to something as commonsense as a question about citizenship on the census—or voter identification. Trust me, it's not "compassion." True compassion would not quit until human trafficking—which always involves sexual exploitation and child abuse—and drug smuggling were virtually eliminated at our southern border.

I was a federal investigator for thirty years. I know that political corruption always comes down to power, money, and votes.

There is no downside to less illegal immigration. And there is plenty of upside to increased *legal* immigration. There's no downside to fewer illegal drugs coming into the country and strangling the criminal cartels in Mexico that smuggle both people and drugs. Again, this is not merely the opinion of someone who took some college courses on the subject; I literally put my life on the line at the border for many years. In many places along the US-Mexico border, and for miles on either side, it's a war zone.

EVERY AGENT'S NIGHTMARE

One day in 1987, while processing an illegal alien in our suboffice, located within the Tecate Point of Entry customs building, I heard dispatch call about a hit on a drive-through sensor just east of the port. The area was notorious for vehicles crossing through an opening in the barbed wire fence at the Mexican border. I quickly placed the alien in the holding cell and hopped in my car to head toward the scene, following another agent who happened to be at the building. As we approached the area, I saw a white van headed north on a dirt trail.

The other agent was in a four-wheel-drive pickup and was able to catch them on the uneven terrain. He lit up his emergency lights, and the van soon stopped. I was about fifty yards behind in my patrol car, but couldn't drive closer because of the rocky path. As I walked toward the van, I could see that the agent was at the front window talking with the driver. The next thing I saw was the van zooming off in a cloud of dust—turning left and dragging the agent, who was tossed around like a lifeless puppet. When he was finally thrown to the ground, the van ran over him with its left rear tire. I was sure he'd been killed.

By now the van was headed straight for me, since I was the only barrier between the driver and Mexico. Since I had no immediate cover of safety, I pulled my revolver and yelled for him to stop. In the next moment I realized my life was also in danger, and I fired several shots as I ran toward an embankment. I know I hit the van because I could see the flash and sparks. Just as I rolled over the embankment, the van sped past.

I ran toward the other agent, certain I'd see yet another dead body.

As I fell to my knees beside him, I was amazed to see he was semiconscious. I asked about his condition, but he only responded with moans. I radioed dispatch for medical assistance, and within about thirty minutes, a life flight helicopter arrived from a San Diego hospital. The agent was banged up badly but released the next day. Both of us could have died that day, and both of us were shaken by the experience.

About two weeks after this incident, a van matching the description of the original set off a vehicle sensor a few miles farther east of the port. The agent responding had the same experience. While outside his car—and unable to take cover—the van spun around and went directly at him. That agent, who happened to be the station's firearms instructor and probably one of the best shots I have ever met, was able to stop the van before it ran over him. He shot through the front windshield, hitting the driver in the head.

The southern border is a war zone. In many places, the only thing that separates the two countries is a flimsy barbed wire fence—or places where a fence used to be. Attacks on Border Patrol are commonplace. There have been 123 Border Patrol officers killed in the line of duty, and assaults on Border Patrol agents are at an all-time high. In fiscal year 2019 alone, there were more than six hundred attacks.

The men and women of the Border Patrol are brave patriots who deal with danger every day. Just a few years ago, a young Campo Border Patrol agent was shot and killed on the very road I often patrolled. Five aliens came to the fence line and stomped around in the dirt, deliberately trying to trigger the sensors. When the young agent responded, they assassinated him, stole his weapon and night vision googles—a useful tool for smugglers—and fled back to Mexico. These five animals ambushed a patriot—a husband and father—for a few hundred dollars' worth of equipment.

There are plenty of good people on the other side of that border. But there are also many bad people. Only those who have never worked along the southern border think that eliminating border security is a good idea. To every congressperson and mayor who verbally attacks Border Patrol agents or ICE, I have a simple challenge. First, shut up. Put on the uniform and work just one shift in the middle of the night. Then tell me what it was like. You know how to reach me.

To some in Congress, having a war zone on and near our border is okay. For those power-hungry people users, caravans of immigrants—including tens of thousands of women and children— are a welcome sight. They don't see people to whom they want to show compassion; they see votes.

But let's get back to the real story. All these policies, rulings, and legal loopholes have a predictable effect on human lives. The innocent, vulnerable, and young are the ones who suffer, including those in the immigrant communities inside our country.

This crisis rests at the feet of Congress. Their failure to address the loopholes, their constant complaining about detaining people until we know who they are and why they're here, their enticements of free health care and a pathway to citizenship for those who come here illegally add fuel to an already out of control fire. If Democrat representatives truly cared about these vulnerable people as they claim, they would fix the issues that result in so much suffering. You know what needs to be done. Let's stop the political wars, the resistance to our president, and fix this. It's just not about enforcing the law; it's about saving lives.

ATTACKING THE PROTECTORS

The Left-wing media, and some in Congress, say that those in Border Patrol custody are mistreated, that the holding facilities are overcrowded and there are sanitary conditions. Representative Alexandria Ocasio-Cortez even claimed that detained women were forced to "drink out of the toilets." Of course that was a lie. But what is her proposed solution? Eliminate the border. I often wonder how she got into Congress. At least she's consistent. From my perspective, every time she says something about immigration, she is wrong.

Once again, ignorant and power-hungry politicians happily ignore the unintended consequences of an open border and demean the vital work of our Border Patrol. It's true that Border Patrol facilities are overcrowded. But instead of looking at the cause of the largest influx of immigrant communities in history, Congress wants to either withhold funding or get rid of the border altogether—or both. Can you imagine what would happen at our border, and happen to our country, if we eliminated the border? In 2019, the Border Patrol took 851,000 people into custody—the most apprehensions in twelve years—and this number does not include the hundreds of thousands denied entry at our border. How many millions of people—certainly a mix of honest folks and criminals from around the world—would walk into our country every month with an open border? And when would it end?

During my time as director of ICE, about 20 percent of those apprehended coming across our border illegally had a prior criminal history. And, of course, when you enter a country illegally, you do violate the law: Title 8 US Code 1325: Improper Entry by Alien.

"People want a fair immigration system. They don't want an open-door invitation for everybody to come at once," a former senator said in 2019. Sounds like an unsurprising position on the issue. The surprising part is that the person making the statement was former Democrat senator Harry Reid.

Our country has changed. Our politics have changed. And our border has changed.

I've worked for six presidents, and I truly respect each and every one of them because they were elected by the people. However, no president has done more to try to secure our border, especially in a time of crisis, than President Trump. What can we do to help? We can demand that our congressional representatives create and pass legislation to secure our borders and remove enticements to act illegally. In November 2020, we can vote and encourage our friends and neighbors to vote. From this chapter alone, you have enough reason to demand law and order on our border.

Congress plays a passive-aggressive game with the Border Patrol and ICE. They vilify them and withhold the funding they need to care for more people—not to mention withholding funds to build a wall that actually works. The elected officials who condemn the Border Patrol and ICE for detention conditions are the same people who refused to answer the agencies' requests for more funds for family facilities.

Six months before the Democrats started complaining about the terrible detention conditions and overcrowding, the chief of the Border Patrol and acting secretary told them it was going to happen. He told them they needed more money for HHS so more appropriate facilities for families could be available. They pleaded and warned for six months, but Congress did nothing. When the warnings became reality, the Democrats blamed the men and women of the Border Patrol. If anyone "manufactured" a crisis, it was the Democrat leadership who willfully ignored the warnings of the people on the front lines.

I will agree that the immigration system is broken, but so is the way Congress conducts business. Congresspeople: You work for us. Start acting like it. Do your duty. Fix the problem you claim to care so much about, and stop demeaning some of the bravest and most selfless people in law enforcement.

Why don't these accusers talk about the more than four thousand lives that the Border Patrol saved just last year? Do those who call agents racist know that over 50 percent of the Border Patrol are of Hispanic descent? No one talks about how these men and women bring toys from their own homes to Border Patrol stations so migrant children have something to play with. Nobody cares about the illnesses many of these migrants arrive here with, and how these agents take illnesses home to their own families because of exposure to airborne sickness and disease. No one wants to talk about agents forced to go through tuberculosis screening because of their exposure to that serious disease.

Who is speaking out for the children who were carried illegally into this country at the hands of a criminal organization, because they were abandoned by their families, while Border Patrol agents, many of whom are moms and dads, console these terrified kids?

In fiscal year 2019, almost 100,000 unaccompanied children were referred to the Health and Human Services Office of Refugee Resettlement. While the Border Patrol is diverting 40 to 60 percent of their personnel away from their national security mission and redirecting resources to provide care, transportation, and related humanitarian functions, the criminal organizations operate with impunity, making millions of dollars every week. These are the same criminal organizations that smuggle drugs and guns into this country—and who have murdered innocent Border Patrol agents. It is a fact that more drugs and criminal aliens illegally cross into the US because the Border Patrol is forced to take agents from the front line to care for sick and abandoned children.

These agents work in an extremely difficult environment and deal with an extraordinary influx of vulnerable people. They do the best they can under the circumstances. Those who attack the professionalism and integrity of those that serve should be ashamed. Border Patrol and ICE agents wake up every day and hear comments from representatives in Congress that they are "Nazis" and "white supremacists" and that they operate "concentration camps."

Do those who make these outrageous statements believe that once you decide to carry the ICE badge or the Border Patrol badge you lose your sense of humanity? There is nothing further from the truth. It is easy to judge when you sit in the ivory tower of Capitol Hill surrounded and protected by Capitol Police. Have these cowardly accusers ever talked with an agent about their job or their opinion about what is happening at the border? Have they ever said thank you to the agents for putting themselves in harm's way for their nation? Have they ever attended an honored burial of a Border Patrol or ICE agent who died doing their job? Have they ever had to console a child or spouse of a fallen officer? Have they ever walked the walls of the National Law Enforcement Officers Memorial, just a few blocks from their congressional offices, and read a few of the more than twenty-one thousand names of the men and women who made the ultimate sacrifice? The memorial includes hundreds of names of Border Patrol and ICE agents, as well as others from their legacy agencies. I have, too many times to count. These brave men and women deserve our highest respect and honor.

There is no question that the recent humanitarian crisis has caused a national security crisis. The border is less protected, and those who want to do us harm will continue to exploit this weakened border. This is one of the many reasons why the president declared a national emergency at the border in early 2019. Because he knows what I know—and what every Border Patrol agent knows. When half of the Border Patrol is no longer on the front line, it creates a national security crisis. If someone wants to come to the US to commit a terrorist act, they're going to take the easiest route to get here. After 9/11, it is very hard for anyone with derogatory information in their background to buy a plane ticket or obtain a visa to enter the United States. If you want to get here, unscathed and unnoticed, you'll enter the same way 20 million others did: illegally, across the southwest border.

A WORD TO MY BROTHERS AND SISTERS OF THE BORDER PATROL

Some of my proudest days were spent serving on the front lines alongside some of the bravest, most selfless men and women I've ever known. To my brothers and sisters on the Border Patrol: Thank you.

Ignore the noise from politicians and the ignorant media. I support you. I know what you face every day. And that's why I want every American to know the real story. I will never stop fighting for you who serve.

FOUR

ANIMALS SMUGGLING HUMANS

Approximately 852,000 persons were apprehended entering the U.S. southwest border illegally in FY 2019. Of these, roughly 550,000 were children traveling alone or children and adults in family groups.
—IMMIGRATION ANALYST STEVEN KOPITS,
PRESIDENT OF PRINCETON POLICY ADVISORS

In August of 2019, the number of pending deportation cases in U.S. immigration courts reached over one million, doubling in just over two years.
—TRANSACTIONAL RECORDS ACCESS CLEARINGHOUSE
AT SYRACUSE UNIVERSITY

Americans don't realize that in order to enter our country illegally, most people need a guide. It's not that the USA isn't easy to find, of course. The brutal reality is that the area south of the border is controlled by criminals who profit from migrants.

I first investigated human smuggling operations in 1985 while with the Border Patrol, in Campo, California, while detailed to the Sector Prosecutions Unit. To say I was ignorant about the practice would be an understatement, but I received a crash course on the job. Here's a quick education on the subject, so you know how illegal immigration actually works at our southern border. I'll be honest with you: The stories and realities of human trafficking are heartbreaking. But please read them. Only when you know the truth can you push back and stop the violence.

HOW SMUGGLING WORKS

If you wanted to walk over the US-Mexico border, there's not much stopping you—in certain areas. Most migrants know the dangers of dehydration or getting lost along the way. But every migrant understands that without the "help" of organized crime, you'd be insane to attempt the journey. You see, nowadays, if a member of a criminal cartel or smuggling organization catches you attempting to cross without paying them, you would be in grave danger. Some migrants have been tortured and robbed for the "crime" of not hiring them. Tragically, paying them does nothing to protect the migrants. Bottom line, the vast majority of people illegally crossing the border have paid the cartels in some way for permission, protection, or transport. Back in the 1980s more crossed on their own, but since alien smuggling has become a billion-dollar business, managed by the largest and most dangerous cartels, the realities have changed for the worse.

Many of the guides know which trails are wired with sensors and know how to spot antennae. They know where there's a wall, and they know where there's an open road to the US. The guides know the Border Patrol's capabilities and coverage. Some actually work on US territory and spy from higher elevations, reporting the location of Border Patrol agents. Smugglers often take their people over the most dangerous terrain, which is why many people get sick or injured and die along the way. They are playing the odds that the Border Patrol will be busy catching many more on an easier path.

Cartels control 100 percent of the Mexican border. Nothing happens on that side of the border without the cartels in the loop. Even the Mexican military and law enforcement know who's in charge, and many are on the take. Illegal immigration is a booming business for Mexican cartels. Yet the mainstream media seems to be ignorant of these brutal realities, while Democrats encourage illegal immigration.

Guides are not hard to find in Mexico, since their organizations basically control the area. Once you find one—if they don't find you first—they'll take you across the border for a certain fee. Usually a portion of the fee is paid in advance, with the balance upon delivery. Once across, you go to a predetermined "load up" spot, usually along a road, where a vehicle will pick you up. In the Victoria, Texas, incident described earlier, the rendezvous point changed, which was a factor in the deaths. Every step is handled by a different group of people, who specialize in their part of the travel.

The next stop is usually the "load house," which is where the smugglers warehouse human beings until they're paid for services. These houses are also operated by specialists who are part of the cartel, and other operators are freelancers, who might work with several different guides. Once you're in a load house, you're held while contact is made with your relatives, future employer, or friend. "Okay, we have your cousin here. Wire five thousand dollars to this account, and we'll deliver him."

There are hundreds of these houses in the United States, and they're often the target of rival gangs and cartels. Consider this: A residence with fifty migrants, each worth five thousand dollars to a smuggler, equals a total value of $250,000, in addition to the cash already there from current payoffs. It's no wonder that these load houses are targets for home invasions and kidnapping. It's like stealing drugs, which can be sold elsewhere, but these rival criminal organizations steal people.

You might not believe that these houses hold that many people, but I've entered many with one hundred and more migrants held captive. *How could the neighbors not know?* you might ask. Most of the deliveries happen in the middle of the night. I've testified in Congress about this issue and even showed video footage of a truck pulling up to a home, and within seconds, dozens of people poured out of the truck and into the house.

When the Border Patrol arrests a large group, the smugglers pose as migrants. We know that at least one or two of them are among the group, but they've already warned the rest about snitching. Not only are the migrants threatened, but the smugglers have contact information for family members on both sides of the border and would take revenge out on them as well. Needless to say, we had a hard time breaking the groups. No one's a smuggler, and they've all been coached on what to say: "I'm just coming here to get a job," or "I'm seeking asylum." By the way, fake asylum seekers only hurt those who truly deserve those protections. President Trump tried to limit asylum claims to those entering legal ports of entry. But think about it: Restricting asylum claims to legal ports of entry—surrounded by federal law enforcement—means people can avoid putting their money and lives in the hands of violent cartels. Of course, the administration was sued and the order was reversed, enticing more people to work with smugglers.

From this point, if everything goes smoothly, you'll either be released or transported to your final destination. Smugglers can arrange transportation to about anywhere in the United States, as long as the price is right. And the price can always increase along the way. At every step and at any moment, chaos, violence, and horrific abuse can occur. And it often does occur. About one-third of women report sexual assault during their journey, according to a recent report by Doctors Without Borders.

For those trying to enter our country illegally, every moment of the journey is fearful.

ANIMALS SMUGGLING HUMANS

On too many occasions, my Border Patrol colleagues and I found dead migrants in the wilderness, presumably dumped because they became sick or died along the way. Smugglers, also called coyotes, won't call for help because it could put their mission in jeopardy. And once one of their "merchandise" (their label, not mine) dies, that person becomes worthless to them. Can you imagine becoming ill and being left to die in the middle of nowhere? This happens to hundreds of men, women, and children every year. Nineteen children died in 2019 during attempted border crossings.

One particular case stands out. A terrified father found our agents on patrol and urged them to help his daughter. He'd broken away from the guides because his daughter fell into a rattlesnake pit along the trail and was left to die. Did the smugglers try to help her? No, they wouldn't risk their lives to save another. What a tragic and frightening way to die. Several agents found her after a brief search, but she had already died. No one should die this way.

We uncovered many smuggling operations that brought Chinese into the US. Many were forced to work for years in restaurants to pay the smugglers, whose fees would increase or simply never end. Again, the threats of criminal cartels should be taken seriously, because they value money and power above human life.

A Guatemalan agricultural worker might pay a few thousand dollars to cross illegally into the US, but people from Asia, Africa, or the Middle East might pay as much as twenty thousand to fifty thousand dollars, depending on who they are and where they want to go. The fees are high because the journey is long and risky for all involved—and many palms have to be greased along the way. Believe me, plenty of bad guys have the money to get here, and they arrive every day.

Thousands of migrant women are kidnapped and forced into the sex trade in order to "pay their fees." Others are smuggled into this country for the sole purpose of prostitution. I only share these facts so more people realize the danger of illegal immigration. Many young people are rightly speaking out about human trafficking in the sex slave industry. But too often, these same well-intentioned people support illegal immigration. They are blind to the fact that illegal immigration actually supports human slavery.

Immigration should not be this way. Legal immigration is a safe, orderly, lawful process. Illegal immigration extracts a huge toll on people and only enriches criminals. The Border Patrol, ICE, and other law enforcement agencies are battling these cartels every day and night, but as you can see, it's a very difficult battle— especially when politicians and media loudmouths blame the very people on the front lines.

SMUGGLING TERROR

If you're a terrorist with the goal of entering the United States, you probably won't be able to travel by commercial airliner. Thankfully, our screening is pretty good. But smugglers don't screen for anything, except cash.

Illegal aliens from almost every country are apprehended by the Border Patrol every year, on both the northern and the southern borders. Here are a few you might be interested to see from their 2018 report: Afghanistan, Algeria, Bangladesh, China, Egypt, Ethiopia, India, Indonesia, Iran, Iraq, Jordan, Kazakhstan,

Nigeria, Oman, Pakistan, Russia, Saudi Arabia, Senegal, Somalia, Sudan, Syria, Tajikistan, Turkey, United Arab Emirates, Uzbekistan, and Yemen. Over one thousand Chinese nationals were arrested by the Border Patrol in 2018, and in just one week of 2019, 153 African migrants were apprehended for illegally crossing the Texas border.

The situation on our borders is not only a humanitarian crisis; it's turned into a national security crisis. In addition to the arrests at our borders, hundreds of suspected terrorists are prevented from entering the US every day through security measures at airports, at ports of entry, and in Panama by our offices there. But what keeps me awake at night is how many we don't catch. And our neighbor to the south doesn't reassure me about our national security.

MEXICAN LAW ENFORCEMENT: IS THERE SUCH A THING?

I always want to give the benefit of the doubt to law enforcement officers, foreign and domestic, but I've had over three decades of experience interacting with those who wear the badge in Mexico. Certainly there are countless dedicated and honorable cops over the southern border, serving in unimaginable conditions. However, the fact is that we can't always count on Mexican law enforcement, including the Mexican military, because many of them are corrupt. Many are paid by the same cartels that traffic in human beings.

HOW HUMAN SMUGGLING HURTS ALL OF US

It's painfully obvious to every Border Patrol agent that smugglers hurt those they guide and their family members. Now you know what we've known for decades.

Trafficking hurts immigrant communities. When a bad guy illegally enters this country, does he move to an affluent neighborhood and get a management job at a tech firm? No. He lives in immigrant communities and preys on their weaknesses—especially on other illigal aliens in the neighborhood.

Women and children are hurt and killed at rates that would sicken any compassionate person. Smuggling is a sadistic crime.

The practice of hiring a coyote to cross our border brings chaos and lawlessness, and that's not what this country is about. *Why should we allow cartels to operate here? Why aren't we fighting them with every means at our disposal?* Their very presence hurts our dignity as a country and should be unacceptable to every American. Organized crime is operating and thriving in the United States because those on the Left allow it. Illegal immigration is not a victimless crime.

OPERATION ICE STORM

I was a Border Patrol agent in Campo, California for four years, from 1984 to 1988. I then was promoted to special agent in 1988 and transferred to Phoenix, where I served until 1997, assigned to the Alien Smuggling Division. In 1997, I became a supervisory special agent and then the deputy assistant district director for investigations (ADDI) in 1998. In 1999, I was promoted to ADDI in San Antonio. I later transferred as the ADDI in Dallas, a much larger office. Soon after that, DHS was created and ICE was born. When it comes to patrolling the border and investigating horrific crimes, I've seen it all—more than I ever wanted to see. But I was there to serve and knew I was making a difference.

In the eighties and nineties, smuggling organizations began to get even more greedy. The prearranged fees were often doubled once the illegal alien was transported to the load house. For example, if a family agreed to pay $5,000 for a niece's journey to Chicago, the coyote might call and say, "We have her here in Texas, and the fee is now $9,500." If the family protested or said they couldn't pay, the coyote would respond in various ways. Some threatened to kill the person. Others threatened torture. Many even put the illegal on the phone and asked them to beg—and some begged while being tortured.

Some paid the increase. Others died. And the smugglers got richer. There was a war within our border. The homicide rate went up almost 50 percent in one year in Phoenix, and the majority were related to human trafficking. On November 4, 2003, a shootout erupted on Interstate 10 in Casa Grande, Arizona—about fifty miles south of Phoenix. Rival gangs of coyotes, who often stole each other's "human cargo," found each other while speeding down the highway in broad daylight. Those in a van opened fire on an SUV and pickup truck. You can only imagine the panic that other drivers also traveling on the roadway must have felt.

When officers arrived, they found four people dead at the scene. Four men traveling in the pickup died. Two other people were injured, including a woman in the SUV who was wounded by gunfire. The attack also caused a three-vehicle wreck that seriously injured one person.

Residents couldn't ignore the problem anymore. Smuggling cartels were destroying Arizona. The local news media couldn't ignore this latest example of gang warfare, and the nightly news finally started reporting about alien smuggling, shootouts, murders, and home invasions linked to illegal immigration. The Phoenix police found so many tortured and murdered people—including those killed in rival kidnapping attempts—they called ICE for help. In November 2003, the White House announced Operation ICE Storm, which was an unprecedented multiagency initiative led by ICE to combat human smuggling and the violence it generates. Once again, I was sent there to oversee the operation and investigative strategy of a dozen federal, state, and local agencies. The success of the investigation in Victoria, Texas, kept my name on the new ICE director's mind. When they needed someone to go out and manage another crisis, I was called. As always, I would salute and get to work. The big downside was that, once again, I would be detailed away from my family for even a longer period. This time, for nearly eighteen months.

In Phoenix, one of the many tactics we used was to simply put our message out: "If you or a family member is in trouble, you can call ICE for help." The cartels are the bad guys; we're the good guys. It worked. People called and gave us the locations and cell numbers of smugglers—and we went to work. As our momentum grew, we decided to take our investigations to the next level.

WHY NOT BEAT THEM AT THEIR OWN GAME?

Back in the late eighties, while I was a supervisory special agent in Phoenix, we asked ourselves how we could best attack these human trafficking operations. Our answer raised a few eyebrows, mine included.

We decided to open up our own load house. The method of smuggling operations was well known to us, so we decided to go into business for ourselves and infiltrate the cartels. We rented a large house in Phoenix, placed hidden cameras everywhere except the bathrooms, and started working our contacts. We also used video cameras and monitored everything 24/7 to make sure everything was safe for the people inside—both undercover agents and the aliens. We contracted with various smugglers to hold their groups until payment was made. The operation allowed us to identify the drivers and smugglers—and we also gained full access to crucial information like delivery addresses, phone numbers, and everyone paying or receiving a fee. This operation broke new ground and put a huge dent in the illegal alien industry.

Operation ICE Storm was such a success that when I transferred to San Antonio as the ADDI the next year, we set up a larger operation in Houston. We learned lessons from the Phoenix operation, such as how to obtain high-quality photos of each alien and coyote without raising suspicion—a necessity for later arrests. We didn't have good identifying photos from the Phoenix operation, and it hampered some arrests. In Houston, we decided to put a poster on an inside wall of the back entrance to the house, where each alien entered at night. It happened to be a poster of a beautiful woman with very little clothing. We placed a pinhole camera behind the poster. As you might guess, every smuggled alien locked eyes with the poster for a few seconds when they entered the house. *Click!* We had them.

As load house operators, we not only got to know the various criminal players, but since we had the role of contacting the aliens' relatives and friends to arrange payment, we knew where each was headed, and our database blossomed. As our evidence grew, we were able to arrest cartel members at all levels of the smuggling operation. And I'd like to think we saved lives in the process. Phoenix and Houston were such successful operations that we dismantled several alien smuggling organizations. I was even called to testify on Capitol Hill about our successes.

DO YOU SUPPORT HUMAN TRAFFICKING?

The vast majority of those crossing the southern border illegally are aided in some way by smugglers, who work for violent criminal cartels. Smuggling people into the United States only strengthens these animals and hurts those in this country—in ways we'll discuss in detail in future chapters.

Astoundingly, the criminal penalties for alien smuggling are often far less than the penalties for drug smuggling. As a result, many drug smugglers get into the alien smuggling business, because it's less risky and hugely profitable. Illegal immigration puts millions of dollars into the coffers of Mexican cartels every single day. Today, as you read this chapter, at least $1 million went into the hands of human traffickers.

Again, some well-meaning people believe the answer is to simply eliminate the border. That's like saying we should legalize all drugs in order to reduce drug arrests. Look at what's happening in Los Angeles, San Francisco, and New York City. When they remove penalties for drug possession, shoplifting, and defecating in the street, you get more of those behaviors and more chaos. Who suffers? Everyone. We need to remind those who claim to care for illegal aliens—especially our elected representatives—that there are safe and legal ways to work in the United States, find asylum, and become a citizen.

Those who support illegal immigration support human trafficking.

FIVE

MAKE IMMIGRATION SAFE AND LEGAL AGAIN

America's last major overhaul of our legal admissions policy was 54 YEARS ago. Think of that.
—Tweet from President Donald Trump in May 2019

Only 12 percent of all legal immigrants to this country are granted access because of skill or employment.
—President Donald Trump in May 2019

A few months ago, I struck up a conversation with a cab driver on the way to the airport. He recognized me and asked if I'd mind talking about immigration. I'm happy to have a friendly conversation with anyone, so I agreed.

The driver went on to tell me that he was originally from an African nation and legally came to the US as a student, graduated, and became a resident alien. He later studied and became a US citizen. As soon as he achieved resident alien status he began the process of getting permission for his wife and his two kids to move here. You could hear the frustration and sadness in his voice. "And it could take several more years before they join me!" He shared his sincere love and respect for this country. "The proudest day in my life, other than the birth of my children, was the day I became a citizen." Then he turned, looked me in the eye, and said, "And I did it the right way. I followed the laws."

Talk about "family separation." He followed the rules, is a productive member of our country, and has been separated from his wife and kids. In addition to driving a cab, this man held two other jobs while he interviewed for a job to put his college education to work. I've said many times that I cannot blame anyone who wants to be part of the greatest country on earth, but you can't disrespect our laws; you can't have it both ways. Our legal system is part of the reason this country is so great.

"I have tried to do the right thing," he continued. "But every day I hear about thousands of people who come here illegally. Why do they get to stay? Why do we financially support them, when my family can't even come here to live with me?"

I didn't really have an answer for this man. I tried to explain how the asylum process is exploited, and how our Congress has no interest in fixing it because they're too busy trying to destroy our president and maintain the non-policy of open borders.

It takes years—sometimes a decade or more—to become a citizen. Legal immigrants stand in line and do the right thing, while others cheat the system and even lie to gain entry. Where's the compassion for the immigrants who play by the rules? Yes, how the United States deals with illegal immigration is a mess. But the *legal* immigration system is also broken.

HISTORY—AND INSANITY—REPEATS ITSELF

In 1986, Congress passed the Immigration Reform and Control Act (IRCA) and President Ronald Reagan signed it into law on November 6 of that year. The legislation made it illegal to knowingly hire illegal aliens and established penalties for employers. The IRCA also legalized most illegal aliens who arrived in the US before 1982. At the time, I was a Border Patrol agent in California.

Of course, the American people were told that this law would fix the problem and were assured that Congress would now address border security. But the IRCA failed to address the legal status of the children of illegal aliens. In 1987, President Reagan created an executive order to legalize the status of minor children of parents who were granted amnesty under the previous immigration overhaul. Some estimated that this order affected 100,000 families, but I believe that was only a fraction of the real number.

What could possibly go wrong? In 1988, I became a special agent in Phoenix, and I was about to find out.

For my first assignment, I worked on the immigration fraud unit, specifically IRCA fraud. The legislation specified workplace enforcement but conveniently left out any provision for resources. No additional agents were hired to actually enforce this new law. How many businesses are in the US, both large and small? How can we possibly ensure they are playing by the rules? With our current staff, we couldn't even scratch the surface. Not only that, the law didn't really have teeth. The most rampant abuse of the law—and the border—involved the Special Agricultural Worker program, which was as complicated as you might imagine. The simple part? Fraud was rampant.

Illegal aliens abused the system, and so did many agricultural employers. To qualify, illegal aliens had to provide proof they harvested fruits, vegetables, or other perishable crops for at least ninety days in a one-year period that ended in May 1986. At the time, the Immigration and Naturalization Service expected half a million applications, but the actual number of applications quickly doubled. It was so easy to commit fraud that thousands who clearly had never worked on a farm in their life applied. Even if an applicant was found to be in the country illegally, or if they were a wanted criminal, the information wasn't shared between the division of the agency that accepted the applications and the division tasked with enforcing the statute and investigating possible fraud.

Employers were required to complete a Form I-9 for each employee and verify two items: the true identity of the employee and their legal authorization to work in the US. For citizens, this would simply mean presenting a driver's license and Social Security card. The employer would complete the form, attesting they saw the documents, and have it on file in case the INS ever inspected the business—which was as unlikely as a Leftist Democrat volunteering to build a border wall.

Many employers didn't even check authorizations, and illegal aliens could easily buy fake documents at a flea market. The result? Most illegal aliens continued to work illegally, and if the business was inspected, the employer would say they had no way of knowing the worker's documents were fraudulent. The INS investigator would have to prove criminal intent, which was almost impossible. Some farmers actually sold letters vouching for an immigrant's work history. Of course, there were no work records to verify employment because before IRCA, there was no I-9 form and most illegal aliens were paid under the table. Can you see how easy it was to commit fraud and buy your way to legal status? IRCA was supposed to fix illegal immigration and stop illegal employment, and it did the opposite. Some farmers had fewer than one hundred employees but sold thousands of letters, creating a new cash crop.

In 1994, I was one of the lead agents on an Arizona case called Desert Deception. My partner and I began to see a common relationship among many of our targets. Numerous undercover operations and informants, who infiltrated smaller criminal groups, led us to Las Vegas and the organization known as the League of United Latin American Citizens (LULAC)—a national organization that is very active in support of Latino causes. While outside the LULAC office in Las Vegas listening to the wire on one of our informants, we heard frequent interruptions to our audio signal, which we guessed was due to another signal being recorded at the same time. We would soon learn that the Los Angeles field office had a parallel investigation, which also led them to LULAC. We joined forces and combined our investigations. At first, there was competition between the two offices and some pretty intense infighting, but we eventually worked very well together. I befriended the lead agent from Los Angeles, and we're good friends to this day.

In the end, we successfully convicted Jose Velez, the national president of LULAC, for his involvement in amnesty fraud and conspiring with other so-called immigration consultants to create and supply fraudulent documents to illegal aliens.

I'll spare you further details, but here's the point: The government creates a program that they say will fix the issues, but in almost every case, the legislation or policy does not include resources for enforcement. And trust me, because these rules are written without real input from the men and women of the Border Patrol, ICE, or other frontline law enforcement, there are always loopholes big enough to drive a van through.

The I-9 form is still used today, and they have developed a system to help employers verify authenticity called E-Verify. And it should be no surprise that Congress has not mandated its use by employers. Can you see a trend here? Congress really doesn't want to fix our immigration problems.

Let me be blunt. I've served under six presidents and too many congresspersons to count. It's always the same.

Congress or the president unveils new legislation and promises "everything will be fine now" as they smile and pat each other on the back.

The American people hear a news report and believe the law will have an immediate and lasting effect—whether they agree with it or not.

The people who deal with the new rules and are supposed to enforce the new laws discover that, once again, there were no provisions to fund enforcement—or to address the new complications and opportunity for fraud the legislation created.

Nothing changes. In fact, the situation gets worse.

At least it's always been the same, until this president. There's a lot of work to be done on immigration and border security. But every step President Trump has taken has included more input from law enforcement and more resources to carry the policies out on the ground. When it comes to legal immigration, we've taken some steps in the right direction.

Here are my top recommendations to improve our legal immigration system.

BREAK CHAIN MIGRATION

What would you guess is one of the biggest drivers in who legally immigrates to the United States? Here's a hint: In the past thirty years, chain migration has accounted for more than 60 percent of immigration here. Okay, I know that's more than a hint, but would you have guessed it was that high?

Every year, we give permanent green cards to over 1 million people. For many, the only basis is being related to someone here—whether that person is a citizen or not. And the connection is not only parent or child. The existing chain migration policy extends to all branches of the family tree, resulting in an uncontrollable increase in legal immigration. Here is how it works. The original immigrant who is admitted into the US is sometimes allowed to bring a spouse or minor children. But once he or she becomes a US citizen, they can petition for their parents, adult children, immediate family, and so on. *Immediate family* can be interpreted widely, as you might guess. Under current law, green card holders can sponsor their spouses and unmarried children for permanent residence—just like naturalized and native-born citizens. And United States citizens can also petition for residence for their parents, siblings, and married adult children.

We must stop extended-family chain migration but continue to allow spouses and minor children to join their family member who followed the rules and legally immigrated. The family household is the building block of our society, and we must support policies that keep this unit intact.

DO YOU PLAY THE LOTTERY?

I don't gamble or buy lottery tickets. But our country gambles its fortune and future every day. The Diversity Visa Lottery admits about fifty thousand immigrants per year, many with no connection to the US, minimal education, and no job offer. Because other governments—including those hostile to our country—choose who is eligible, this program has also been exploited by national security threats.

The Immigration Act of 1990 established the lottery, with the intention to further diversify our immigration population by bringing more people from less-represented countries. It sounds nice, like most well-intentioned liberal policies, but being "nice" ranks far below the safety, security, and economic well-being of our country. Sound harsh? About 21 percent of legal immigrants are allowed here by chance. That's right: Other countries create the pool of eligible people, and the ones who get to immigrate are selected at random. Why would we allow this? Our universities don't run admissions this way. Companies don't hire this way. And even the best nonprofit charities make sure those receiving aid actually need it. Why would we invite people into our country who we know nothing about?

Every year, thousands of international students come to this country for the best education in the world. Many want to stay and apply their talents and skills here, for the benefit of this country, but are forced to go back to their home country because our immigration code is outdated. Why not give these people a better shot if we need their skills and talents?

We must, once and for all, end the Diversity Visa Lottery.

OVERSTAYING THEIR WELCOME

Where were you when you heard about the terrorist attacks on the morning of September 11, 2001? I was on the way to work at my office in the San Antonio Office of Criminal Investigations for the INS, when my wife called my cell phone and asked, "Are you watching the news?"

"No. Why?"

"An airplane hit the World Trade Center."

"What? How did that happen?"

Then she gasped. "A second plane just hit."

I knew immediately that this was no accident. As soon as I got to the office, the bosses pulled us all together and we mobilized. I sent agents on a military flight to the East Coast to help. The FBI had the lead in the investigation, but the Immigration and Nationalization Service was able to open many doors for them because of our unique access to immigration information. The FBI needed to immediately talk with many people who were in the US under visas, and we already had relationships with the suspects. Those foreign nationals could stall other federal agencies, but not immigration authorities.

As we worked closely with the FBI for many months, we learned that four of the hijackers had overstayed their visas. Fourteen of the terrorists entered the US on six-month tourist visas, four entered with business visas, and several visa applications had "detectable false statements," according to the 9/11 Commission Report.

One of the main legal ways people begin a life in the United States is through a visa. A visa is temporary permission to visit, live, and sometimes work in a country. But many—hundreds of thousands, actually—overstay their visa every year and simply remain here.

According to the Department of Homeland Security, there were over 700,000 visa overstays in 2017. You might wonder, *Is there a penalty for overstaying a visa?* Basically, no—which only adds to the problem. But it gets worse. There is almost no program to find, apprehend, and deport those who take advantage of this country's generosity. There are some checks for criminal history, but mostly the federal government looks the other way. And as you can imagine, the number of those here illegally because of visa overstays is several million, which creates a daunting task for law enforcement.

ICE simply does not have the manpower to follow up. The hundreds of thousands of overstays are run against various databases by ICE, and those who might seem to present a threat to national security are targeted for capture and removal by Homeland Security Investigations of ICE. The remaining will be run against criminal databases, and those with a criminal history after entry will be prioritized for arrest. Those, along with the tens of thousands of other criminals arrested all over the US and languishing in our jails, continue to be the priority. Those who overstay their visa and have no other criminal or national security issue will remain on a backlog until they are encountered, usually as part of another criminal arrest or another unrelated operation, such as a worksite raid.

This issue is extremely frustrating for ICE agents, because they simply do not have enough officers to seek out violators or the cells to put them in after arrest. Those who enter illegally on the border and are immediately arrested will be detained and removed, but an entire population of visa overstays seldom get arrested and detained. Those who excuse visa abuse claim that deporting hundreds of thousands of violators would hurt our economy. But, as usual, they ignore obvious solutions. Here are a few.

First, we need to establish a bond program for worker visas. This bond would work like a deposit: Pay a fee before the visa is issued, and receive the money back when you return to your home country. If nothing else, this would at least fund enforcement operations. The bond needs to be high enough to make a difference. It must be higher than someone would pay a coyote to be smuggled to the US from that country, because many of the people who enter the country on a visa have always intended to stay and never leave. They simply chose this route rather than to hire a smuggler. The Border Patrol catches a much higher percentage of people at the border than we do those who violate their visas. It's all about the end game and making the legal process as clean as possible.

Second, overstaying a visa should be a crime. Again, many who receive a visa have no intention of leaving. These people knowingly abuse the process by lying on official government documents and committing perjury. There must be consequences and deterrence to illegal activity. If there was never an intention to leave at the end of the authorized stay, that—in my mind—is no different than entering the country illegally, which is a crime. Let's take our hands off the scales of justice and hold people accountable to our laws.

Third, expand the guest worker visa program if clearly justified. If we need more temporary workers, let's increase the number of legal employees. Of course, the first two recommendations would need to be in place for this to function correctly. Legal workers mean fewer illigal aliens paying criminal cartels, since they can simply go through a port of entry with their money, health, and dignity intact. This also decreases the likelihood that people will overstay their visa to find employment. Again, there must be a clear, substantiated need for more legal immigration and guest workers that can be validated and communicated to the American people with complete transparency.

Finally, mandate the E-Verify program with some minor improvements. If we did this, those who overstay their visas could not obtain employment, and this would disincentivize them to violate their visa terms and stay here illegally.

THE MERITS OF IMMIGRATION

Can you imagine our country without an illegal immigration crisis—with a legal immigration and visa system that actually strengthens the United States? I can. Because it's possible.

As ICE director, I attended several meetings at ICE headquarters and the White House on the issue of immigration. I was honored to review and give feedback on the Trump administration's policy and proposals, along with many other advisors. Simply running the agency was more than a full-time job, but I wanted to not only lead ICE with excellence; I wanted to actually find solutions to the immigration crisis. So, it was a lifelong dream to work with an administration that wanted long-term solutions to fix the problems we face.

The United States is in competition with the rest of the globe. Our immigration system needs to keep pace, for the good of every citizen—and future citizen. As overseas outsourcing, robotic automation, and artificial intelligence continue to replace American jobs, we need to apply some simple logic to the debate.

Only one out of every fifteen immigrants is admitted in the US on the basis of their skills. Our immigration policy can be summed up like this: "Whoever can get here, can stay here—along with their entire family; we'll figure the details out someday." If you don't agree with that assessment, ask an ICE agent.

However dysfunctional and unfair, the current system has been able to help some terrific people immigrate here. The United States has also continued to be the most compassionate country on the planet, offering refugee status to more people than any other nation. We may or may not need more legal immigration, but we need lawful and organized ways to make that happen if needed—and make our country stronger in the process. Our immigration policy and practices are actually hurting our country.

Most progressive nations have some sort of merit-based immigration. Why? Common sense. Merit—a set of criteria established to benefit the country based on its demographics and needs—will never be the sole criteria for legal immigration, but should at least be a part of how we decide who gets to come here. Yes, I know that the mere thought of our country having a say in who gets to live here will trigger those on the Left. But the United States needs to focus on merit-based immigration, for the benefit of its citizens and the future of our country.

A continual, massive flow of low-skilled workers drives down wages, raises unemployment, and drains social programs. The current system actually incentivizes illegal immigration because those who game the system often receive the same benefits as those who follow the legal process. In fact, as in the case of my cab driver friend, illegal aliens often receive more perks.

We've got to stop rewarding bad—and illegal—behavior and award green cards to those who can help build this country. We all want more people who will successfully assimilate and financially support themselves.

Why don't we select immigrants based on talent, specialized vocational skills our country needs, proficiency in the English language, and high academic achievement? Other countries do. It's possible to have a transparent process that levels the playing field and benefits the United States.

Only 12 percent of all legal immigrants to this country are granted access because of skill or employment. If you factor in the huge number of illegal aliens entering every year, that effective number is even smaller. In contrast, in countries like Canada, Australia, and Japan, more than half of all immigrants are accepted based on skills and employment. Again, no one wants to keep moms, dads, and their minor children apart, and the Trump administration's plan accounts for this.

A May 2019 briefing from the White House lays out the percentages of various countries:

> United States. 12%
> Canada 63%
> New Zealand 57%
> Australia 68%
> Japan 52%

In 2019, President Trump proposed that we change that percentage from 12 to 57 percent, with 30 percent of legal immigration based on family and 10 percent based on humanitarian reasons. His plan would not change the number of green cards issued, and it still supports visas for the nuclear family. Basically, this means taking back control of our immigration for the good of our country.

What do you think would happen if we had simple, clear criteria for entry into our country—including an appreciation for civics and the English language? Would it help our nation economically? Socially? Educationally? If we had a truly secure border, we could even increase the number of people we allowed to immigrate here. I'm all for that.

The health and security of our country depends on strong families, respect for the law, skilled workers, and young people. The president wants to establish a sane immigration policy that is transparent and intentionally brings in more people who can contribute to our success. Several renowned economists reviewed this plan and agreed it would increase our nation's GDP while increasing wages for the American worker.

A WIN-WIN FOR AGRICULTURE

I grew up in farm country and understand the seasonal nature of agricultural work. That's why I enjoy shocking the Left with my work to improve *and increase* our Seasonal Agricultural Worker policies. The H2A program allows a limited number of worker visas, and I pushed to expand it to include dairy farms. Yes, I understand that milking cows is not "seasonal" work. As I learned firsthand as a teenager, a cow is milked twice a day, every day. But I also understand many of our dairy farmers are struggling and need additional employees, and the low unemployment numbers make it even more challenging for them to find employees. Farmers are the backbone of this country. When a family farm fails, a part of this nation dies. My view is that if we're bringing in workers legally through this system, why not expand the program to help farmers with their year-round work?

Expanding the H2A program in this way will also reduce the number of people paying a cartel to illegally enter the US and keep our farmers far away from anyone involved in human trafficking. Again, this is a simple fix to expand legal ways to live and work in this country.

If there's a need for ten thousand extra harvest workers, I'd rather see them come in legally. That's ten thousand people who are not paying a criminal cartel and putting their lives and families at risk. Again, let me be clear: There must be a justified need for these workers and reassurances that they would not displace legal workers who are already here. Immigration and guest worker programs must help our country.

Many Democrats want to talk about increasing the number of visas and other legal immigration opportunities, but without real border security it becomes a game—a game in which the United States is always the loser. And we've played that game for decades.

WHAT YOU DON'T KNOW ABOUT DACA

Most people think Deferred Action for Childhood Arrivals, better known as DACA, is about high schoolers and college-educated children. But to qualify for DACA, you only need to go online and sign up for one online course. Eureka! You're in. Too many of these DACA kids aren't kids; many are in their thirties and have criminal histories. In November 2019, the US Citizenship and Immigration Services (USCIS) reported that 12 percent of DACA recipients have an arrest record—including some for violent crimes.

More problematic is the DACA program explicitly allows criminals to receive work permits, Social Security accounts, and other benefits such as driver's licenses. DACA also allows those convicted of up to two misdemeanors a free pass from deportation. Multiple misdemeanors arising out of the same action and taking place on the same day can count as one misdemeanor.

Even though DACA allows illegal aliens with criminal convictions to be qualified by the agency that runs it, USCIS admitted to Congress that it does not electronically track criminality among DACA recipients. USCIS also admitted it does not track how many DACA applications have been denied because of gang affiliation and other criminal acts. At the start of DACA in 2012, DHS terminated approximately 1,500 applicants due to criminality or gang affiliation. With 1,500 DACA terminations, it is clear that DACA standards are insufficient for the purpose of protecting legal residents of the United States.

Don't get me wrong: Many in the DACA program are fine young adults who live and work in the United States and contribute greatly. But we must clear up the misconception that it's the law. DACA is not a law; it was an executive order created by President Obama. DACA does not give anyone legal status; it merely defers their status for a temporary period. And that's the third myth about DACA: It's "temporary." That's true, if you also consider death and taxes temporary. The order was supposed to be a Band-Aid to prevent children from being deported for a period of two years. Instead of working with Congress to truly fix the issue—and prevent future issues—President Obama signed an order. And since 2012, it's been too painful to pull that Band-Aid off.

My professional opinion, which happens to usually be the same as my personal opinion, is that President Obama didn't have the authority to make that executive order. He actually seemed to agree with that point of view in a statement he made months before signing the order. However, since the Supreme Court has DACA in their sights, we will see what they say. Practically speaking, deferred action is a form of prosecutorial discretion. Law enforcement and prosecutorial authorities have long used prosecutorial discretion, but it's always based on a case-by-case analysis of the factors, and a decision based on those unique factors, in this context, "Should the person be removed since they are here illegally, or are there extenuating circumstances?" The problem with DACA is that prosecutorial discretion was decided on an entire population at once.

If a cop pulls you over for speeding, they can write you a ticket—or not—depending on many circumstances. ICE also can use a form of deferred action, and agents exercise it every day. Let's say you have a final deportation order, and ICE arrests you. You can say, "I'm going through some medical treatment, and I'd like to finish this before I leave." In many cases, you'll receive deferred action, if you are not a criminal or public safety threat. We're going to defer your removal until your treatment is finished. I once handled a case of a man who was being deported because of a visa overstay. He asked if he could stay an additional thirty days until his child graduated high school. Of course, we deferred action.

Situations like this should only be handled on a case-by-case basis, because every case—and every person—is different. But DACA was a one-size-fits-all policy that created as many problems as it was designed to solve. Of course, the same people who applauded President Obama's executive order have spent the last three years criticizing President Trump for actions that reverse those Obama-era policies.

If the Supreme Court decides that President Obama did have the authority to create DACA, then I believe that a president should have the same authority to end it. If they decide that the president erred in creating DACA, there will be a huge legal gray area—and many innocent immigrants will be stuck there. As he's done since his first day in office, President Trump should then urge Congress to negotiate a legislative solution. Either way, the high court's ruling is an opportunity to improve legal immigration.

If and when Congress considers a DACA solution, they should not propose a "clean DACA fix" and not address the underlying reasons that this situation occurred—putting millions of young people in legal limbo. We must demand that legislation also closes the pipeline that allows millions of people, including children, to come into this country illegally. If Congress puts another Band-Aid on the problem, we're destined to repeat the crisis over and over. We've sent the message to the world that if you hide out long enough, we will reward your illegal behavior. It's no coincidence that family unit crossings surged shortly after DACA was created in 2012. In the past few years, thousands of parents brought children into this country illegally, "through no fault of the child," and they will be our next DACA population if we don't fix the issue once and for all. It's time to change our message and our laws. American citizens have paid a high price for the inaction of our elected officials.

POLITICIANS: I'M PAYING THE PRICE. WILL YOU?

Any legal immigration must maintain or increase wages for legal citizens and residents. Amazingly, some people—including some Republicans—don't champion this outcome. I have a message for politicians. Stop prioritizing your political future above the strength and security of your country. Stop basing your policy decisions and talking points on how it will play out in your next election. For once, on the issue of immigration, do the right thing for this country. You are in Congress to do a job for the American people. Stop putting yourselves first, and put citizens first.

When I was ICE director, I received countless death threats. So did my family. We've had protesters outside our home, screaming the worst insults you can imagine. We've received detailed, credible threats of violence, and still do. People threatened to kill my child.

When I was appointed ICE director, several people told me to be more guarded and less candid. "It will hurt you in the confirmation process, because you'll make too many enemies."

I told them, "If I have to change who I am, what I stand for, or what I know is right based on thirty years of law enforcement, they can vote no and let me retire. I didn't come looking for this job; they came looking for me."

Unlike many in Congress, and unlike too many mayors and county officials, I will not sell out for a vote, and I will not sell out for a job. I will never sell out this country, and I will never shut up when I see wrong. I will defend the men and women of the Border Patrol, ICE, and all law enforcement until the day I die. They are the finest 1 percent this country has. Those who've paid attention since my retirement know my commitment. I put myself in the backseat and put my country in the front seat, and my family has done the same—many times. They've sacrificed so much. But we do what we do to make our country safer, for everyone—including immigrants and including the people who hate my guts.

All I'm saying is that I expect our elected officials to take the same stand. Legislating and enforcing our laws should be their number-one priority—not growing their power and bank accounts. Right now, as a former ICE director, do you think I have more or fewer opportunities in the marketplace? Most would be shocked at the truth. In our "cancel culture," it's very difficult for those who simply speak up for the law.

In October 2019, I was scheduled to be on a panel discussion at the University of Pennsylvania. Before the event a petition was circulated that read, in part, "Under Homan, ICE continued to be a violent organization responsible for terrorizing immigrant communities . . . Inviting Homan as a guest speaker contradicts Penn's claim of being a sanctuary campus." The hosts of the event informed me and gave me the opportunity to cancel. "Hell no," was my reply. "I will not allow anyone to silence me. I have earned the right to speak about this issue because I served in that arena for decades."

Thankfully those who invited me did not bow to the pressure, but once the event began, protesters disrupted the meeting to the point where security was forced to clear the room.

I won't be bullied. The ones who want to shout down speeches will remain ignorant. They call us Nazis, but the Nazis were the ones who shut down free speech. Think about it.

Will you stand with me? Will you speak up? If you see a wrong, say it's wrong. If you believe in a solution, make noise about the solution. And don't ever shut up. Do you have the number of your senator, representative, governor, and mayor in the contact list on your phone? Take just a few minutes and enter them. Then call them, and respectfully inform them that you are for legal immigration if it benefits the United States but against illegal immigration. Be heard. This is your country, too.

SIX

ILLEGAL EMPLOYMENT: BIG PROBLEM, SIMPLE SOLUTIONS

17.4 percent of the U.S. labor force consists of foreign-born persons.
— BUREAU OF LABOR STATISTICS 2018 REPORT

100%

THE PERCENTAGE OF ILLEGAL ALIENS WORKING IN THE
UNITED STATES EITHER USING STOLEN IDENTITIES OR BEING
PAID UNDER THE TABLE

Let's be honest. Economic opportunity is the main force driving migration. Therefore, since illegal employment is a magnet for illegal immigration, it only makes sense that the United States government find ways to take that magnet away. Notice I specified "illegal employment." If we need temporary workers or those with specialized skills, let's find ways to employ those individuals legally. Taking away the enticement of illegal, "under-the-table" employment will not only cause a reduction of illegal migration, but it will also save lives and take money away from criminal cartels.

WE'VE BEEN HACKED

When I was in charge of the Dallas office of investigations for the INS, my wife and I were in the process of buying a house. This wasn't our first house, but any new home is exciting for a family. Days before we were scheduled to close on the purchase, the mortgage company called to tell us there were unpaid electrical bills from a Fort Worth utility company, which had been turned over to a collection agency, and this caused a red flag in our credit check. We never lived in Fort Worth and were not familiar with the utility, and as far as we knew we had excellent credit. We discovered that someone had used my wife's Social Security number to open several credit accounts. We had to jump through legal hoops for weeks to prove the debts weren't ours. It was a burdensome process, and I was angry. Someone stole from us, and the theft caused a lot of stress and extra work—and delayed our financing. I have a friend in California who also had her identity stolen, which ruined her credit rating and almost destroyed her business. Her bank accounts were shut down and finances were locked up for months. Even after six months, she still had problems restoring her finances, credit rating, and business reputation.

Most Americans don't understand that many illegal aliens steal the identities of US citizens by using their Social Security numbers. Identity theft is rampant within illegal employment. Many citizens have had their identities stolen and their credit rating ruined by this practice. The next time a person questions why ICE is conducting a worksite operation, they need to ask themselves a few questions. How many US citizens' identities were stolen by those who were arrested? How many of those people had their credit ruined, and what will it cost them to get it back to normal? How much money did the company that hired those illegal aliens fail to pay the US government in required taxes, unemployment insurance, and workers' compensation? Many large-scale worksite enforcement operations involve a criminal investigation into the company for tax evasion.

Illegal employment is not a victimless crime. Addressing the issue is a key component to solving the crisis at our border.

Employers do not hire illegal aliens out of the goodness of their hearts. They hire illegal aliens so they can pay them less and work them harder—often under terrible working conditions. Many employers use the threat of calling ICE if the illegal employees complain. Employers often hire illegal aliens so they can undercut their competition.

After a recent storm damaged my home's roof, I had to call six different roofing companies until I found one that would guarantee a legal workforce. The company I contracted had just two employees, a father and a son. The father explained to me that years prior he had a much larger company that employed many people. But he could not compete with the companies that used illegal aliens in their workforce—and who worked for much less. As the years went on, this employer had to lay off his legal-citizen employees. The once-thriving business now consisted of a father and son who only did roof repairs, not new or replacement roofs. As you can imagine, his income was slashed, along with the jobs he used to provide for his crew. This is another reason that ICE must conduct worksite enforcement operations and hold employers accountable to our laws. Policies like this are not anti-immigrant; they are pro-citizen and pro–legal immigrant.

ENFORCE EMPLOYERS

In my many years as an agent and investigator, almost every illegal alien I arrested had some sort of job in the United States—either unlawfully employed at a legitimate business or making money while involved in criminal activity. When I became ICE director, I knew illegal employment was a major draw for those seeking to enter the United States. I immediately pledged to increase worksite enforcement by 400 percent, and we accomplished the goal in our first year. We actually hit 420 percent and saw tangible results.

Years earlier, ICE began auditing Asplundh, a nationwide provider of tree removal services. Investigators amassed evidence that the company accepted bogus driver's licenses, green cards, Social Security numbers, and other counterfeit identification—and discovered Asplundh employed several thousand unauthorized workers. In 2017 the company was ordered to pay $95 million because of their intentional scheme to employ illegal aliens. They have since implemented a photo ID system with facial recognition software and investigate every complaint regarding unauthorized employees. "We accept responsibility for the charges as outlined, and we apologize to our customers, associates and all other stakeholders for what has occurred," said CEO Scott Asplundh in a press release on their website. There's so much more that can be done, but my experience shows that enforcement is possible, and it helps our citizens.

The solutions are, as usual, straightforward and based on common sense. We must continue to step up worksite enforcement, which requires Congress to fund more law enforcement positions for ICE to actually investigate companies across the nation. And because identity fraud is so rampant with illegal alien employment, the Social Security Administration (SSA) database must be updated to make sure people are not using someone else's Social Security number. And the fix is not rocket science. Whenever the SSA finds someone using a number that doesn't belong to them, they can immediately send that information to ICE for follow-up. Not only would this provide ICE with valuable leads to investigate criminal behavior, but it would also help address identity theft. This fix is so simple; however, the current Democrat leadership has yet to even consider this provision of the president's proposals.

But most important, E-Verify needs to be mandatory. E-Verify is an online system that compares information on Form I-9 (Employment Eligibility Verification) to US Department of Homeland Security and Social Security Administration records to confirm authorization to work in the US. By law, Form I-9 must be filled out by every employee; it requires documented proof of identity and work eligibility. The problem is, E-Verify is still optional for most businesses. It's mandatory for citizens and businesses to file taxes, so why don't we require businesses to make sure their employees have the legal right to work here? This program would save tens of millions of dollars per year in enforcement operations by making it much more difficult to use fake identities. E-Verify is the best tool available, and it currently prevents a significant amount of unauthorized employment.

PROPOSED WORKSITE ENFORCEMENT STRATEGY

In 2018, when I was ICE director, we developed a worksite enforcement strategy consisting of three major operations, which are still used today.

Operation Inbound targets employers who operate in secure areas that could be exploited by terrorists. These include commercial cargo ports, seaports, airports, water treatment plants, and more. We simply must know the true identities and backgrounds of people who work in these facilities. These businesses are directly connected to our nation's critical infrastructure.

Operation Backtrack revisits and audits businesses previously identified as an egregious work site. These companies have a history of illegal employment and we need to keep checking on them.

Operation Hammer focuses on the service and construction industries. These two industries employ the largest share of unauthorized workers.

To be effective, all three of these operations must be carried out together. Employers must be fined, so there is an incentive to comply with verification. If you hit a construction company but don't arrest the illegal alien employees, they will simply go to work for another construction company. That is why you have to address entire industries, not just a few businesses within an industry. Policies like this will result in higher wages for legal employees, less unfair competition, the correct level of tax revenue, and fewer cases of identity theft.

Some say that making E-Verify mandatory would shut down meat-packing plants because many who work there are illegal aliens. First, I enjoy a hamburger as much as anyone—okay, maybe more—but that's a stupid reason not to enforce our laws. Second, if these jobs can't be filled by citizens, let's expand legal options if clearly needed. And while we're at it, we can even expand employment opportunities for those truly seeking asylum, since many cases take years, and legitimate asylum seekers want to work and assimilate.

LET'S TALK TURKEY—AND SOLUTIONS

Tyson Foods came to the table and asked ICE to help them comply. Today they have a legally compliant workforce because they adopted E-Verify and worked with ICE to address the issues. In August 2019, ICE raided several poultry-processing plants in Mississippi— not affiliated with Tyson—and arrested 680 employees who were suspected of working illegally. Where are these companies supposed to find good employees? They should call Tyson and ask how they did it or, better yet, work with ICE and its Mutual Agreement between

Government and Employers (IMAGE) program, and they will find a way. IMAGE assists employers in developing a more secure and stable workforce. As part of IMAGE, employers receive education and training on proper hiring procedures, fraudulent document detection, and the use of E-Verify employment eligibility verification program. Tyson did it the right way by working with ICE and taking advantage of the vast resources the agency makes available to employers. It's possible, and beneficial, to have a legal workforce.

I truly believe E-Verify is the best system available for helping companies comply with immigration law, but I also propose improvements to the system, because there are loopholes. I have recently been discussing such updates with a friend of mine. Mark Reed was a senior leader in the INS. After retirement, he led Tyson's efforts to become 100 percent compliant, which helped shape the future of the IMAGE program and overall employer compliance programs.

Before I explain the proposed solutions, let's examine the current landscape.

The government is always looking at different methods to improve their programs, and one of many is an app-centric option to streamline the Form I-9 process and E-Verify inquiries. The technology will relieve some of the responsibility imposed upon employers to comply with regulatory requirements by placing more of the burden on prospective employees. However, I believe this solution alone will not improve the integrity of E-Verify, since it can still be gamed. A recent proposal introduces the third-party app vendors focused on process efficiencies for employers, but it does not attain the primary goal of eliminating identity fraud, which is the weakness of the current system. The recent worksite enforcement operation by ICE in Mississippi clearly demonstrates that employers may participate in E-Verify but still hire unauthorized workers who simply provide false identities. Industries notorious for the employment of unauthorized workers know that E-Verify cannot effectively detect identity fraud.

Several years ago, the government designed and implemented a process that would eliminate the vulnerability of E-Verify to detect identity fraud. The process, called Self-Check E-Verify, is available online at CIS.gov as an element of the E-Verify program. Self-Check allows a person to confirm his or her own employment eligibility. After gathering information online from the individual concerning their identity, Self-Check compares it with various government databases to verify identity and work eligibility. The process includes anti-fraud techniques, including multiple-choice questions that could be correctly answered only by the true owner of the identity. Some banking institutions already use this type of technology. As a matter of fact, just the other day, while updating my online bank account, I had to answer some questions about previous addresses and what vehicles I've owned. The technology works well. Expansion of Self-Check could eliminate the vulnerability to identity fraud. It's so simple and potentially effective that there must be a catch, right?

Employers are currently prohibited from integrating Self-Check into their hiring process due to some initial concerns by the government. I hope those agencies will work to overcome any concerns with the integration. If they can, employers could easily integrate Self-Check into their existing hiring process. After the acceptance of a job offer, the applicant would be provided private, on-site access to Self-Check to verify their eligibility to work. The E-Verify response could be instantly conveyed electronically to the employer as well as the applicant.

The Self-Check process satisfies the regulatory requirements and purpose of Form I-9 and can effectively bar the employment of unauthorized workers, while removing much of the burden from the employer in the verification process, which will cause more employers to engage. However, if successful, this effort could bring strong political and economic backlash. A measured and strategic approach, with attention toward preserving a legal labor pool would be essential—namely, an expanded and transparent guest worker program. Bottom line: This proposal would dramatically reduce the enticement to come to the US illegally but would open even more doors for those who want to work here legally.

If you're asking yourself, *Why does Tom Homan care, now that he's retired?* my answer hasn't changed in over three decades, and it's the reason I wrote this book. If you had seen and experienced the terrible tragedies that I have throughout my career, you'd understand why I couldn't just walk away. I have to stay engaged and work for change. I have to hope that we can secure our border and protect America, and by doing so, save many, many lives. I don't want to hear one more news story about human trafficking or an immigrant who died. I don't want any agent to kneel next to the body of a dead child and wonder why we haven't fixed the crisis. I love my country with all my heart, that is why I dedicated my life in service to it. I also love life. We can save many lives if we take action.

Instead of endless emotional arguments, name-calling, and gridlock in Washington, DC, let's focus on thoughtful solutions. If more Republicans and Democrats would discuss practical, detailed proposals, the public would come together, and we could solve the crisis. I know that sounds a little idealistic, but my faith is in you and our fellow citizens who want to move forward. And in my experience, when valid solutions are presented, those who are not serious about border security are exposed.

The next time you hear any of the current Democrat presidential candidates clucking about a fifteen-dollar minimum wage, remember that their policies result in more illegal aliens and create an environment where US citizens are forced to work for less money, pay more in taxes, and send their kids to more crowded schools and hospitals. If these candidates really cared about people making a good wage, they would be for mandatory verification of legal employment. But instead, they advocate for open borders and benefits for illegal aliens.

Whether it's a construction site or a meat packing plant, illegal aliens often work in very dangerous conditions, for low wages and with no overtime or benefits. This issue is not only about enforcing the law, protecting American businesses, and keeping wages up—it's about preventing the abuse and exploitation of illegal aliens. Many of those smuggled into the country are forced to work months or years to pay off their smuggling debt. I've had cases where companies have called ICE to arrest the illegal workers a day before payday, so they wouldn't have to pay them. Of course, we would always ask the employer to issue checks for any amount owed during the operation, but it didn't always happen.

I don't want honest, hardworking people to be deported; I'd much rather they found a way to work legally. The president's proposals, which I helped frame, create additional ways that non-citizens can find legal employment in this country.

SEVEN

ILLEGAL IMMIGRATION: FACTS, FEELINGS, AND FIXES

Out of every 100 credible fear claims, on average, only about 12 result in a grant of asylum by an immigration judge.
—THE DEPARTMENT OF JUSTICE'S OFFICE FOR IMMIGRATION REVIEW 2019 REPORT

67.3 Million in the United States Spoke a Foreign Language at Home in 2018.
—FROM A CENTER FOR IMMIGRATION STUDIES REPORT BASED ON CENSUS BUREAU DATA

W hy should it be easier to enter this country illegally than it is to enter an airport for a flight?

Why should those who don't follow the law when they step into the United States be treated any differently than those who try to board a flight without a ticket or identification?

When it comes to the debate about illegal immigration, we need to address the truth. Human emotion is a factor—and rightly so—but only when we base our policies on objective facts can compassion be directed for long-term solutions.

END ASYLUM FRAUD

We know that smugglers coach their clients on what to say when they reach the border, and this often involves advice on how to game our liberal asylum procedures. In my time at ICE, I saw plenty of intelligence reports and interviews of illegal aliens who admit to being coached. In 2015, I made a trip to the Phoenix ICE office to investigate. While I was there, agents were loading two buses with women and children who recently crossed the border—and were playing the asylum fraud game. Dressed in casual clothing, I stood by the entrance of the bus and asked the women (*en español*) why they were coming to this country. Each one said they were coming to join their husband, who was already working and living here illegally. There was not one whisper of fear or persecution. The responses didn't surprise me at all. Throughout my career, this has always been the main reason for women and children to come to the US.

If you doubt my perspective, let's look at what the International Organization for Migration (IOM) says about this issue. IOM is an intergovernmental organization and a related organization of the United Nations. They released a study in 2017 that found that the primary reasons why migrants came to the United States were economic (64.1 percent), family reunification (9.1 percent), and fleeing violence (3.3 percent). The IOM study concluded that a total of just 6 percent of illegal aliens from Guatemala seek entry based on alleged violence, threats, insecurity, or discrimination.

Other studies, including a 2019 publication by Creative Associates International, a nonpartisan global development NGO, found similar percentages. "Nearly two-thirds of all survey respondents have a relative living abroad, 75 percent of those relatives have lived in the U.S. for 10 years or more, and about 25 percent for over 20 [years]."

The Department of Justice's Office for Immigration Review (EOIR) released a fact sheet in 2019 titled "Myths vs Facts about Immigration Proceedings." Here are a few pertinent ones.

MYTH: Most aliens who claim a fear of persecution in expedited removal proceedings have meritorious asylum claims.

FACT: Out of every 100 credible fear claims, on average, only about 12 result in a grant of asylum by an immigration judge.

MYTH: Most aliens who claim a credible fear of persecution are asylum seekers.

FACT: On average, at least half of aliens who make a credible fear claim and are subsequently placed in removal proceedings do not actually apply for asylum . . .

MYTH: Few aliens fail to attend their immigration court proceedings.

FACT: Forty-four percent (44%) of all non-detained removal cases end with an *in absentia* order of removal due to an alien's failure to attend a scheduled immigration court hearing.

In recent years, there's been an exponential increase in asylum claims. In 2019 there was a backlog of over 270,000 cases with US Citizenship and Immigration Services (USCIS) and over 482,000 in the immigration court system. Nearly half of the immigration court's pending caseload involves applications for asylum, and they received over 200,000 new asylum cases in fiscal year 2019—the highest number ever. Compared to 2013, asylum applications received in immigration courts have increased by over 165,000, whereas asylum grants have increased by only slightly over 9,000. In 2019, less than 20 percent of total asylum applications were granted, and for Central Americans the number is closer to 10 percent. Finally, the number of in absentia removal orders issued by an immigration judge—because an illegal alien failed to appear in court—nearly doubled from 2018 to 2019. And these numbers only reflect cases that were filed with the court. Almost half of Central Americans who claim asylum at the border never file a case with the courts at all.

Our current asylum process is, frankly, full of false claims by people who know they can game the system. Before President Trump implemented the Migrant Protection Protocol (MPP)—which is also referred to as the "Remain in Mexico" program and mandates that many immigrants wait in Mexico for their asylum hearing—most people who claimed asylum were released before their scheduled appearance before a judge. The vast majority never appeared at their hearings. Once these fake asylum seekers are released, they disappear into society. Even with the MPP in place, many are still released into the US. This is especially common with citizens of Mexico, because we can't return a citizen back to the country from which they claim protection until it is ascertained that no real threat exists. I also have concerns about how long the MPP will remain in place while groups on the Left continue to push courts to end the policy.

At the time of this writing, the US immigration court system has a backlog of more than 1 million cases. Because the system is so overwhelmed, a single case takes an average of almost seven hundred days to complete, and the Democrats in Congress aren't likely to increase funding to speed up the process. And the case schedule might as well be seven hundred *years*, since court dates are often skipped by immigrants and removal orders are often ignored. We need a real solution.

The first and most important step we must take is to raise the initial bar to pass the first asylum claim interview. Nearly 90 percent of the initial asylum claim interviews on the border result in a "pass"—meaning that the person's claim is deemed worthy of future consideration. But at the end of the process, approximately 90 percent who claim asylum at our border do not receive positive relief from the judicial system. The vast majority of those who actually show up and see a judge will not receive relief because they don't qualify. Nine out of ten pass their first interview, but nine out of ten fail in the end when scrutinized. It only makes sense to make the pass or fail bar at the border interview closer to the judicial requirements for asylum.

This simple change would stop as many as 90 percent of fraudulent and frivolous claims from clogging up the system and hurting those who truly qualify. Let's not miss this point. There are people in this world who are truly escaping fear, persecution, and death from their home governments, and they need our help. That help does not come as quickly as it can when there are a million cases in line before them. It's simply not fair to those who are actually escaping oppression. Those who promote loopholes in our generosity are actually hurting our country and those who deserve our care. This is a point you seldom hear, but a basic humanitarian one. Remember that when you hear Democrats, including presidential candidates, talk about "compassion" on the border.

REMAIN IN MEXICO

The Migrant Protection Protocol is an important step in regaining control of our southern border, so let's take a deeper look. When "Remain in Mexico" was implemented in 2019, the number of illegal aliens crossing our border illegally was at unprecedented levels. The MPP requires that certain foreign individuals entering or seeking admission to the US from Mexico—illegally or without proper documentation—may be returned to Mexico to wait outside the US for the duration of their immigration proceedings. During that time, Mexico provides them with all appropriate humanitarian protections.

A January 2019 press release on the Department of Homeland Security website (DHS.gov) reads, in part:

MPP will help restore a safe and orderly immigration process, decrease the number of those taking advantage of the immigration system, and the ability of smugglers and traffickers to prey on vulnerable populations, and reduce threats to life, national security, and public safety, while ensuring that vulnerable populations receive the protections they need.

Historically, illegal aliens to the U.S. were predominantly single adult males from Mexico who were generally removed within 48 hours if they had no legal right to stay; now over 60% are family units and unaccompanied children and 60% are non-Mexican. In FY17, CBP apprehended 94,285 family units from Honduras, Guatemala, and El Salvador (Northern Triangle) at the Southern border. Of those, 99% remain in the country today.

Misguided court decisions and outdated laws have made it easier for illegal aliens to enter and remain in the U.S. if they are adults who arrive with children, unaccompanied alien children, or individuals who fraudulently claim asylum. As a result, DHS continues to see huge numbers of illegal migrants and a dramatic shift in the demographics

*of aliens traveling to the border, both in terms of nationality
and type of aliens—from a demographic who could be
quickly removed when they had no legal right to stay to one
that cannot be detained and timely removed.*

*In October, November, and December of 2018, DHS
encountered an average of 2,000 illegal and inadmissible
aliens a day at the Southern border . . . Record increases in
particular types of migrants, such as family units, travelling
to the border . . . have overwhelmed the U.S. immigration
agencies, leading to a "system" that enables smugglers and
traffickers to flourish and often leaves aliens in limbo for
years. This has been a prime cause of our near-800,000 case
backlog in immigration courts and delivers no consequences
to aliens who have entered illegally.*

The MPP was long overdue because I know what asylum is and
what it isn't. If people simply understood the basic rules of asylum,
most would support the MPP, too. However, the Left confuses the
issue by spreading the lie that all those who come to our southern border are asylum seekers. Asylum is about escaping fear and
persecution from your home government because of your race,
religion, political affiliation, or membership in a specific social
group. Therefore, if someone claims asylum from Honduras and
enters Mexico, haven't they escaped their government's persecution? Mexico, in addition to other nations in Central and South
America, are designated "first entry" countries for asylum seekers.
Let's be honest about asylum and focus our efforts on those who
truly meet the criteria.

In my days as a Border Patrol agent, we could process an illegal alien from Mexico within twenty minutes, and after accepting a
voluntary return, the person would be returned to Mexico through

a port of entry within minutes. All that changed when—thanks to Democrat policies—the majority of those crossing were "family units," and mostly from Central America. These people are detained, but usually released into the shadows of this country, where they disappear and wait for the next DACA or amnesty to roll around.

There are only about three thousand designated family beds to deal with the almost fourteen thousand family unit arrests during the peak months, which means most will be released and never spend a day in detention. Out of the most recent 100,000 family units who have been ordered removed after due process, less than 2 percent have left the country. In June 2019, the acting secretary of DHS testified about a recent study that revealed that 90 percent of all family units failed to show up in court after being released at the border. The MPP will help to ensure that those who claim asylum and want to receive due process will actually see a judge. I agree that anyone entering the US has a right to have their case reviewed by a judge. But can we also agree that after due process, if ordered removed by a judge, that order needs to be followed up and enforced? Can we agree that our laws should be followed so those abusing our country's generosity do not ruin the system for those truly in need?

Again, from the DHS statement:

The MPP will provide a safer and more orderly process that will discourage individuals from attempting illegal entry and making false claims to stay in the U.S., and allow more resources to individuals who legitimately qualify for asylum . . .

Certain aliens attempting to enter the U.S. illegally or without documentation, including those who claim asylum, will no longer be released into this country, where they often fail to file an asylum application and/or disappear before an immigration judge can determine the merits of their claim. Instead, these aliens will be given a "Notice to Appear" for their immigration court hearing and will be returned to Mexico until their hearing date.

While aliens await their hearings in Mexico, the Mexican government has made its own determination to provide such individuals to stay in Mexico, under applicable protection based on the type of status given to them.

Aliens who need to return to the U.S. to attend their immigration court hearings will be allowed to enter and attend those hearings. Aliens whose claims are found meritorious by an immigration judge will be allowed to remain in the U.S. Those determined to be without valid claims will be removed from the U.S. to their country of nationality or citizenship.

"Remain in Mexico" will dramatically reduce the number of people taking advantage of our law and stop enticing people to falsely claim asylum. Instead of being released in the US—where most will not show up for their court date—they will remain outside the United States until their claim can be evaluated by a judge. All this frees up the men and women of our Border Patrol to focus on security.

The only remaining question should be, *Why wasn't this done ten years ago?*

"ANCHOR BABIES" AND BIRTHRIGHT CITIZENSHIP

Did you know the United States has a policy that makes anyone born in the country a legal citizen? This policy began in the late 1700s and was eventually expanded to include African Americans.

In 1868 the Fourteenth Amendment to the Constitution opened citizenship to "All persons born or naturalized in the United States, and subject to the jurisdiction thereof." Many believe that this provision was intended to address the full citizenship of former slaves and not intended to promote "birth tourism."

A 2019 report from the Center for Immigration Studies estimates that 72,000 United States–born children are delivered to foreign students, foreign tourists, and foreign visa workers every year. This number is in addition to an estimated 300,000 births by illegal aliens each year.

Birthright citizenship is a very emotional and controversial issue, and the mainstream media thinks that any discussion about the policy leans toward racism. In their view, anyone who questions the practice is a white nationalist—and God help you if you use the term *anchor baby*. I disagree with their assessment, of course, because I am neither a racist nor white nationalist. I'm a career law enforcement officer who's seen things almost no other American has seen or would want to see. I have been recognized by numerous courts as an expert witness in the area. Being a recognized expert does not mean you are a racist, bigot, white nationalist, or the other derogatory label the media or certain members of Congress want to slap on you.

Here's an objective fact: The policy of birthright citizenship is a problem for our country because it is being abused and puts lives unnecessarily at risk. The practice, whatever its origins and intentions, creates huge incentive for people to come here legally and illegally. In many cases, the adults involved are deliberately taking advantage of the situation for their own benefit—which adds additional strain to all aspects of our immigration crisis. Whether you agree with birthright citizenship or not, you must admit that it drives illegal immigration, which results in death, sexual abuse of girls and women, and the bankrolling of criminal cartels. If you disagree, you're simply ignoring reality.

While the director of ICE, I worked with a very talented advisor who understood the whole illegal immigration issue very well. Like me, Jon Feere has been called various names by people less educated on the issue and by people who don't know either of us. He wrote several papers on the issue of birthright citizenship and birth tourism, and we've had many discussions around these policies and needed adjustments. Some of his research follows.

In 2015, Feere testified in Congress and offered these points:

Every year, 350,000 to 400,000 children are born to illegal immigrants in the United States. To put this another way, as many as one out of 10 births in the United States is now to an illegal immigrant mother. Despite the foreign citizenship and illegal status of the parent, the Executive Branch automatically recognizes these children as U.S. citizens upon birth, providing them Social Security numbers and U.S. passports. The same is true of children born to tourists and other aliens who are present in the United States in a legal but temporary status.

On the issue of chain migration:

A child born to illegal aliens in the United States can initiate a chain of immigration when he reaches the age of 18 and can sponsor an overseas spouse and unmarried children of his own. When he turns 21, he can also sponsor his parents and any brothers and sisters. Family-sponsored immigration accounts for most of the nation's growth in immigration levels; approximately 2/3 of our immigration flow is family-based.

Only 30 of the world's 194 countries grant automatic citizenship to children born to illegal aliens. Of advanced economies, as rated by the International Monetary Fund, Canada and the United States are the only countries that grant automatic citizenship to children born to illegal aliens. No European country grants automatic citizenship to children of illegal aliens.

Eminent legal scholars and jurists, including Professor Peter Schuck of Yale Law School and U.S. Court of Appeals Judge Richard Posner, have questioned whether the 14th Amendment should be read to mandate such a permissive citizenship policy. Nevertheless, the practice has become the de facto law of the land without any input from Congress or the American public.

The Department of Justice routinely investigates the practice of "birth tourism," which has become very popular with wealthy Chinese citizens and those from affluent countries. Specialized travel agencies even offer all-inclusive packages—costing up to $50,000—for those wanting to take advantage of the policy. "Maternity hotels" and related services are a multimillion-dollar business. Some estimate the number of babies born here by "birth tourists" to be between thirty thousand and sixty thousand per year—each being granted full US citizenship. The practice is a legal gray area because there's no law against having a baby in this country, but lying about the reasons for a visit can constitute visa fraud. Regardless, this loophole is exploited by rich and poor from every country.

From my three decades of enforcing immigration law, I can tell you that having a US citizen child is a goal of most illegal aliens that I have encountered. And I have learned there are several reasons why illegal aliens chose to have a child born in the United States. First, because the child is born a citizen, they believe the child will someday be able to help them become citizens. Second, they can collect welfare benefits for that child, which opens up benefits the parents would otherwise not be allowed. Third, they have children here because they believe it will save them from deportation. And certain members of the media and Congress have argued that this should be the case. Many Democrat members of Congress agree that an illegal alien with a US citizen child should simply be ignored by immigration officers. That sort of talk only entices more to enter this country illegally—and have children here. Giving birth to a child while here illegally—and while ignoring a federal judge's order to leave—should not give anyone immunity from the laws of this country, and it certainly shouldn't give automatic amnesty. We must restore the issue of birthright citizenship to its intent and not continue to encourage people to risk their lives in this practice.

In 2015, I oversaw a few national operations where ICE sought out family units who entered the US illegally and were ordered removed by a judge after receiving due process. The combined operation was called Operation Border Guardian and Border Resolve. Yes, we did this during the Obama administration. But when President Trump had ICE continue the practice, the media and the Democrats went nuts. Regardless, we searched for these families across the country and found that almost half of those young mothers had already given birth since arriving here or were pregnant when we found them.

The United States is the greatest country on earth, and I can't blame anyone for wanting to come here and enjoy the benefits of citizenship. ICE investigates birth tourism, but with the current crisis the issue has not been a priority. If the president or Congress simply ended the policy of birthright citizenship, it would immediately solve a huge problem. Regardless of the final decision, the men and women of ICE will enforce whatever laws are on the books—as they've always done. Now that you understand the painful consequences of this practice, you and I can make our voices known to our elected officials.

EXPLOITING OUR GENEROSITY

In November 2019, a group of illegal aliens staged an elaborate hoax in SeaTac, Washington. They fabricated a violent crime scene and reported a robbery, claiming that two Samoan men had attacked them at a restaurant. Police questioned the alleged victims and quickly discovered their lies. They also uncovered their motive: to game our compassionate immigration rules which allow special "U visas" for victims of violent crimes as well as those who help police solve real crimes. To avoid deportation, and gain legal status, these criminals deliberately took advantage of programs designed to help those truly in need of our compassion and generosity.

"Participants decided they would pin this fake robbery on two Samoan males," the local sheriff noted. "Not only do we have a hoax, we have a racially motivated one."

We covered visa abuse in the previous chapter, but this is another aspect of illegal immigration. Bad people—people you and I would not want in our community—take advantage of our laws every day, while law-abiding people pay the price.

The Center for Immigration Studies reported in 2018 that 63 percent of noncitizen households accessed welfare programs in 2014—compared to 35 percent of citizen households. They also found that "Compared to native households, noncitizen households have much higher use of food programs (45 percent vs. 21 percent for natives) and Medicaid (50 percent vs. 23 percent for natives)."

I'm sure we agree that our country must continue to provide for those in need. But I hope we can also agree that illegal immigration does put a huge drain on our resources. Our current practices are simply not sustainable and only entice more illegal activity.

ASSIMILATION FRUSTRATION

Our national motto is "E pluribus unum," or "Out of many, one." I celebrate the "out of many" aspect of this country. But we must also focus on the goal of becoming "one." Illegal immigration hinders assimilation. People here illegally are less likely to learn the English language and become active members of our society because no one demands it. Illegal aliens are also less likely to report crimes and cooperate with law enforcement because of fear of being deported— which is not based on fact. Political leaders and the media have spread the lie that ICE is a heartless organization that seeks to arrest and remove anyone—including victims and witnesses of crime.

In their quest for power, some Democrats use fear to divide this country. We must address the need for assimilation and improve our programs to help people embrace what makes America great, so they can enjoy the same freedom and opportunity as other residents.

So many family groups entered the country illegally last year that our schools are running short on English as a second language educators. During my time with ICE, some of the migrant caravans carried the flags of their home country. Would you wave the flag of a country that was persecuting you?

Assimilation makes our communities safer and more cohesive. It helps immigrant children do better in school and opens up a wider career path. A country with one common language is more unified—and stronger—than a country with two or ten languages. I'm not arguing that immigrants should abandon their heritage or not celebrate their traditions. They should remain proud of their heritage and native language, but they can also embrace the culture and language of their home country. The Left and proponents of open borders don't want assimilation or incentives to learn English, because they want to keep immigrants separated into a political faction. Democrats can then pander to them and even spread falsehoods and lies regarding Republican policies and law enforcement actions. The purpose? To gain political power.

Naturalized immigrants have expanded the roster of legal voters by over 700,000 foreign-born citizens—every year. Naturalized citizens made up more than 8 percent of votes cast in the 2018 election, based on US Census Bureau estimates. These immigrants followed the law, and I welcome them. What troubles me is how the Left has framed the narrative to give the impression that Republicans and conservatives are anti-immigrant. Yes, this is part of the Democrats' strategy to gain power.

THE BOTTOM LINE

Most illegal aliens are drawn to the US to obtain employment, reunite with family members who are here illegally, and receive government benefits from welfare to citizenship.

Most are low-skilled immigrants. This is a potential problem based on workforce trends, automation, and outsourcing to foreign countries. Let's reexamine the criteria for who should be allowed to enter.

Many exploit our generous immigration system, which hurts those who respect our laws and follow the rules. Doing the right thing—following the process for legal immigration—should be rewarded and should not be more difficult than violating our laws.

Sanctuary cities allow criminal aliens to remain on our streets and re-offend. This makes our communities less safe and increases the risk to the brave men and women of law enforcement.

Backlogged immigration courts allow illegal aliens to delay or evade removal. During those long periods, they will have children who are granted US citizenship and become integrated with their community, which will make removal even more difficult.

We face unnecessary challenges with quickly removing illegal aliens apprehended at the border—especially under this administration, when our leadership is sued almost daily by those who want open borders.

We have insufficient resources to enforce immigration laws in the interior of the US. More interior enforcement positions are needed. There is no real border security without an interior enforcement mechanism that is capable of seeking out those who are here illegally and enforcing the orders handed down by the courts.

Our legal immigration system currently favors low-skilled or no-skilled immigrants through extended family chain migration. Immigration based on merit has been successful in many flourishing countries.

The solutions are simple: Enforce all current immigration laws within the United States as a top priority. Secure the border by deterring and promptly removing illegal entrants. We need new legislation to confront illegal immigration and improve the legal immigration system.

We cannot continue to release criminal aliens back into our communities.

We cannot continue to bring individuals here with no regard to their skills or merit.

We cannot continue to look the other way as hundreds of thousands of people break our laws.

We cannot continue to run a justice system crippled by debilitating immigration backlogs.

We cannot continue to simply hope terrorists don't take advantage of our generosity and welcoming tradition.

Do I have to say it again? There's no bigger fan of immigration than me. But illegal immigration is harming our country. And when I say "our country," I mean not only our society but our neighborhoods.

Illegal immigration creates chaos, not community. And this country needs more community and less chaos.

EIGHT

BLURRED BORDERS AND CRIME

Non-U.S. citizens, who make up 7% of the U.S. population (per the U.S. Census Bureau for 2017), accounted for 15% of all federal arrests and 15% of prosecutions in U.S. district court for non-immigration crimes in 2018 . . . Ninety-five percent of the increase in federal arrests across 20 years was due to immigration offenses . . . Of non-U.S. citizens prosecuted in U.S. district court in 2018, 0.3% were prosecuted for first-time illegal entry; 99.7% were prosecuted for something else.

Trips on Air Force One are always interesting, as I learned on my first flight as acting director of ICE. I certainly wasn't a frequent flyer, but as a kid from upstate New York, I never dreamed I'd have a seat on that airplane, nor did I imagine I'd find myself in the Oval Office or situation room of the White House.

In June 2017, I had the honor of accompanying President Trump on a flight to Long Island, New York, where I'd make a few opening remarks, along with Representative Peter King, before the president took the stage. We were there to do a public gathering with local sheriffs and police, along with law enforcement from the state. ICE officers and agents also attended in great numbers. The president wanted to make remarks and thank local and federal officers for their work combating MS-13 gangs in Operation Matador, which was a great success on Long Island. Several hundred gang members and associates were arrested and taken off the street. Many were in the US illegally.

Fun fact: There are assigned seats on Air Force One. The airplane is quite impressive and unlike any commercial airliner. It has conference rooms, private offices, and plenty to eat. The food is great. A few minutes after boarding, a boisterous character strolled up to me and said, "I hear you're the ICE man!" It was Anthony Scaramucci, during his brief time as White House director of communications. "The president loves you and talks about you all the time," he continued.

"Well, that's good to know," I answered.

Mooch continued with something to the effect of "I'm on thin ice right now. Can you throw in a good word for me with the president? It would mean a lot coming from you."

"I'll see what I can do," I replied, and went back to my paperwork.

About twenty minutes after takeoff, a Secret Service agent walked down the aisle and said in a quiet voice, "The president would like to see you in his office." He escorted me to the room, where Stephen Miller, Nikki Haley, and a few others were seated, along with President Trump.

"Sit down, Tom," he said from his desk. "You have some opening remarks today at the event. What are you going to talk about?"

"Do you want to see my notes, Mr. President?" I asked.

"No, no. I saw you on TV a few weeks ago talking about MS-13. You said, 'My gang's bigger than their gang.' I love that. You always have these catchphrases. Do you have one I can use?"

"Just say, 'MS-13 ain't shit; our agents are tougher and stronger. We're going to take them down.'"

Everyone in the room laughed. "I can't, I shouldn't, say that," he said with a smile.

"Maybe try something like, 'Our gang's bigger than their gang,'" I suggested. "We have agents who are serious tough guys, tougher than MS-13. They are no match for us. MS-13 thinks they're tough, but they haven't met tough. My agents are going to take these people out and dismantle their organization piece by piece. They're going to look for them, arrest them, and remove them from this country in record numbers."

Later, at the event, and after Peter King and I delivered our short speeches, the president took the stage. Two of his statements were very meaningful to me.

"So I asked Tom on the plane—he was never on Air Force One—I said, 'How do you like it?' He said, 'I like it.' But I said, 'Hey, Tom, let me ask you a question—how tough are these guys, MS-13?' He said, 'They're nothing compared to my guys. Nothing.' And that's what you need. Sometimes that's what you need, right?"

The president of the United States asked for my input and listened. He brought me up to the podium, shook my hand, and thanked me for my service. I have to admit that was a pretty cool experience—and a moment that confirmed the calling I felt all my life.

His second statement meant even more to me and to the men and women of law enforcement: "I have a simple message today for every gang member and criminal alien that are threatening so violently our people: We will find you, we will arrest you, we will jail you, and we will deport you."

Unless you've served your country on the front lines, you can't imagine what those words mean from a leader. And to see those words backed up by actions is even better. The president was clear. We will now do our job and fulfill the oath we took to enforce the law.

HEROES THEN AND NOW

Later that evening, on the way back to Washington, the same Secret Service agent came to my seat and asked me to follow him to see the president. As I entered the small office and took a seat in front of his desk, I realized it was only the two of us.

"I need to ask you a question, Tom, if it's okay. What do you think of John Kelly?"

"I think John Kelly is an American hero," I instantly answered. "John Kelly's the one who called me when I retired and asked me to come back to work for this administration. I probably wouldn't have taken that call from anyone other than him or you. And he's a great secretary of Homeland Security. Best one I ever worked for. I respect him as much as I do my own father."

"Well, thank you. Good to know." He then remarked about what a great event we had in New York, and his hopes for my continued successes as the ICE director. You don't hear it enough in the media, so let me say it here. The president is truly a friendly, caring, and honest person.

We landed at Andrews Air Force Base, where the president was about to have a news conference in front of the plane. As I drove off the airfield, I tuned the radio to Fox News, just in time to hear him announce John Kelly as his new chief of staff. Do I think that my discussion with the president got John Kelly the job? Of course not. But I've seen it over and over again and experienced it for myself many times: This president asks questions of those who serve— and he listens. Even if you don't support his decision or agree with his thinking, he wants the feedback. To me, every great leader or manager wants feedback from the people who get the job done on the ground. I respect this president for that.

To be honest, I was bummed that we were losing a great secretary of Homeland Security. But I also realized that Kelly could play a bigger role for the president and have a greater impact. As a US Marine Corps general, John Kelly was a patriot—always has been, and always will be. He was decisive and always supported the men and women on the front lines. A few months before this announcement, Secretary Kelly walked into my office and immediately spotted a shadow box on the wall that contained numerous military medals, including the Purple Heart, the Bronze Star with an oak leaf cluster, various paratrooper medals, and campaign medals— along with a patch that read "11th Airborne." He looked at me and said, "Whose are they?"

"They were my dad's. He is my hero."

"Do you know what all these medals are and what they mean?"

"No," I replied. "My dad didn't talk about them much. As a matter of fact, he kept them out of sight for many years and never displayed them."

Kelly walked me through every medal and explained what each meant and what it took to earn one. Then he looked me in the eye and said, "Your dad was a war hero, Tom. Wounded twice during combat and saved many lives." As he was talking, his photographer snapped a picture of us. To this day, I display these medals in honor of my dad, who never bragged about his service. The shadow box is now in my home office, beneath his funeral flag, which was presented by the military at his funeral. Next to the medals is a picture of John Kelly and me, taken as he explained the significance of each medal. That's the best wall of my office, by far.

To this day the president occasionally calls me to get input on various aspects of the border and immigration. On one such call,

I told him I was smoking a brisket for my brother, who was visiting from Florida and had recently retired as a fireman. The president asked to say hi to him, and I handed the phone to my brother. President Trump spent several minutes thanking my brother for his service and telling him how much he respected first responders. He also spoke to our wives and thanked them for putting up with a couple guys who served their community for so many years. This is the president of the United States, not a neighbor or relative. That's the type of man he is. He respects those who serve and will always spend time speaking with them and sincerely thanking them.

I spent thirty-four years studying people for a living, trying to figure out what makes them tick. I can say without hesitation that all the crap they say about this president is nothing more than that—crap! He's not a racist. He's a man who loves his country, and he's doing everything he can to make sure we can keep the America we love—the America we grew up in, as I did in West Carthage. He truly cares about victims of crime and wants to prevent more heartache.

THE HEARTBREAKING FACT ABOUT THESE CRIMES

Sadly, crime is a fact of life, but preventable crimes are often the most heartbreaking. There's a serious epidemic of crime in the United States, committed by people who should not even be in this country. Every crime—murder, assault, robbery—committed by an illegal alien is a crime that could have been easily prevented if we had true border security, closed the loopholes, and enforced the law without apology. As I share some facts and stories about crime, gangs, and cartels, I hope you'll keep that in mind.

Keep this fact in mind as well: Most people in this country illegally are not "bad guys" who terrorize communities, sell drugs, and traffic in human beings, but unless we take this problem seriously, everyone suffers. As ICE director, I went on record and affirmed that if you are illegally in the United States, then you should not be "comfortable" here. Many of the Democrats and the media went nuts. When questioned by a congressman, I told him, "That's the way it's supposed to be." You shouldn't be comfortable when breaking the law. If you speed down a highway, you should be concerned about getting a ticket. If you lie on your taxes, you should worry about an audit. If you violate the laws of this country and enter illegally, you need to be worried. I don't want to live in a country where people have no concern about violating the law. We are a nation of laws, and if you want to be part of the greatest country on earth, you need to respect our laws or face the consequences. Again, that's how civilized society thrives.

I can't possibly capture the full picture of needless crime in these pages, but I hope your eyes will be opened, and I pray you'll be emboldened to speak up. As you read this, pause and think about the victims of crimes committed by illegal aliens—and their families and friends. May our voices turn the tide, and may the actions of our leaders prevent needless suffering. To the angel moms and dads, I will always stand with you.

FICTION AND FACT

In October 2019, Osmani Garces-Ortiz was arrested in Arapahoe County, Colorado, on trespassing and drug charges. ICE asked the sheriff's office to detain Garces-Ortiz, but they did not. In less than thirty days, he was arrested by the Aurora, Colorado Police Department on charges of attempted murder in a stabbing incident. As I said, stories like this happen almost every day. "Sanctuary" policies make cities and counties less safe for everyone, regardless of immigration status.

People who are against enforcing immigration laws and those who are for sanctuary cities constantly claim that illegal aliens commit fewer crimes than citizens. And the media—and many Democrats—believe them. They often refer to a 2018 study by the Cato Institute, which wrongly concludes that illegal aliens are less likely to engage in criminal activity. Let's begin by setting the record straight about that report.

I believe the Cato study is flawed and biased and contains misleading conclusions. Other experts and organizations, such as the Center for Immigration Studies, agree. First, the Cato study isn't based solely on crime data from the federal, state, and local crime databases—much of it is based on surveys. Second, their study combines crime statistics from both legal immigrants and illegal aliens, which skews the results. Third, of course a higher number of crimes committed are by citizens, because the overwhelming majority of people in this country are citizens. But when you compare percentages, the truth stands out. According to the Department of Justice's Bureau of Justice Statistics 2018 report, 64 percent of all federal arrests were of non-US citizens.

When I was ICE director, approximately 20 percent of those the Border Patrol arrested for entering the country illegally had a criminal history in this country already. Think about that. One in five people arrested illegally crossing the border had already committed a crime here. And a huge number of those crimes are gang related. Once again, President Trump was right when he said that many criminals cross the border illegally. Many Democrats and Leftists in the media attacked him for it. Maybe they should do some research first and learn the facts.

FOREIGN GANGS ON US SOIL

In 2018, according to Homeland Security Investigations (HSI) 4,818 suspected gang members were arrested, including 796 MS-13 arrests. If you've never heard of the MS-13 gang, their motto says it all: *"Mata, roba, viola, controla,"* which mean "Kill, steal, rape, control."

Quick death is not something MS-13 believes in. They want to terrorize. What better way to create fear and control than to take a machete to their enemies? They are famous for dismembering their victims with machetes, stabbing them hundreds of times, and carving out their hearts. The immigrant community—legal and illegal—fears MS-13 greatly because they're not just a gang that will kill you and your family; they're a gang that will torture and then kill.

When I was a special agent in Phoenix twenty-five years ago, I participated in a gang unit for the INS because local authorities recognized that most of the gang members were in this country illegally. To this day, HSI and Enforcement and Removal Operations—both divisions of ICE—participate on numerous gang task forces across this country. For thirty years, I've been working to take gang members off our streets.

We know that many gang members sneak into this country along with family groups. Many unaccompanied children are also gang members. Remember, when you hear about unaccompanied kids, don't picture a three-year-old crawling across the border—although that actually happens. Most of these "children" are in their teens or are in their twenties and posing as minors. When ICE launched Operation Matador two years ago in New York, we arrested hundreds of gang members—mostly MS-13 and their affiliates. A little over 40 percent of those gang members arrested came to this country as either a family unit or an unaccompanied child. Illegal immigration and the proliferation of gangs are well connected. The reason local law enforcement comes to ICE for our assistance is because ICE can remove the illegal alien from both the community and the country, so they are less likely to return to the community and re-offend.

ICE also has a strong relationship with the government and federal police in El Salvador (the birthplace and home of MS-13). We've assisted in arresting thousands of MS-13 gang members in El Salvador. The prison in El Salvador is full of MS-13 gang members because of the work of ICE.

I was the head of investigations in Dallas in 2002, and we created a huge operation against MS-13. After arrests started snowballing, I did a press conference, along with the Dallas police. Every local network covered it. A few hours later my gang unit supervisor informed me that the local leader of the MS-13 put a hit on me immediately after the TV appearance. I was in the office when notified and immediately had my wife and children moved from my home to a safer location. Our gang task force went back into the streets in force and immediately arrested more MS-13 gang leaders. Within a couple days they ascertained that the leader who put a hit on me fled back to El Salvador because the heat was on and we were looking for him.

We had a picture of the leader, who had typical MS-13 tattoos all over his face. I said many times during my interviews then, and when I was ICE director, "Our gang is bigger than their gang." The ICE gang unit now uses that as their informal motto. I took some heat for that phrase, but I stick by what I said. The law enforcement gang is much more powerful than any criminal gang—especially when the commander in chief supports them. There are over 120,000 federal law enforcement officers in this country. There's no gang that big. My gang in Dallas was bigger, and the leader who threatened me ran away because he knew it, too.

IMMIGRANTS AND GANGS

The illegal alien community has become the perfect target and the perfect recruitment center for gangs because of some of the

Democrats' policies. Illegal aliens are less likely to report crime and gang activity for fear of being deported, even though that fear is unfounded. Sanctuary policies put criminals right back onto the street instead of out of the country or in prison. When a gang controls an illegal alien community, teenagers within that community do not have much of a choice about joining that gang.

The immigrant community is the main source of recruiting for these gangs. They make a lot of money from prostitution, drug trafficking, and coercing immigrant businesses to pay protection fees. It's a big business. MS-13 gangs are operating in almost all fifty states. The United States is a target-rich environment with over 300 million citizens and at least 12 million illegal aliens to threaten and steal from—and the illegal population is often the most vulnerable.

According to Pew Research, in 2017 there were 2.3 million Hispanics of Salvadoran origin in the United States, and the number is climbing quickly. For comparison, the entire population of El Salvador is about 6 million. You can't take blood out of stone. There's not a lot left in El Salvador to steal. Sadly, the Left has opened the door to this gang to terrorize people in this country, and because of this gang's roots in their home country, they can—and frequently do—threaten immigrants in the US with threats of violence against family members in El Salvador.

CARTELS ON BOTH SIDES OF OUR BORDER

According to the Department of Justice's Bureau of Justice Statistics 2019 report, "In 2018, a quarter of all federal drug arrests took place in the five judicial districts along the U.S.-Mexico border."

A cartel at its core is a gang. However, cartels are huge, organized gangs. Cartels operate more like businesses, and they control the northern border of Mexico—and punish those who try to cross the border without their help.

In a recent interview with Breitbart News, my friend and colleague Manuel Padilla Jr., director of Joint Task Force—West, told a story about a recent incident in which cartel members brutally beat a pregnant migrant woman because she did not hire them in her attempt to cross the border. "During November of 2018, there was a young lady that was coming in. I believe she was from Guatemala. She freelanced and crossed into the Brownsville Area of Operations and she did not pay the cartels. This young lady was eight months pregnant. When the agents encountered her, she was beaten up so bad by the cartels, or by criminal organized crime, because she had not paid those dues." He went on to say that Border Patrol agents immediately took the woman to the hospital. The baby was stillborn, and the mother was so badly injured that she needed dialysis.

These cartel and gang members are not animals. They're much worse. During an event I attended with the president, we met with families whose children were tortured and killed by gangs such as MS-13. The president famously referred to these gang members as "animals." When it was my turn to speak, I looked at the president while the cameras were rolling and told him I didn't know why he would refer to the MS-13 as animals—because they are worse than animals. Animals kill to survive; MS-13 kills for the sport of it.

In November 2019, armed cartel members stormed the General Hospital of Salvatierra, Mexico, entered the room of their target and dragged him away. The patient was later found—his body dismembered.

In December 2019, just an hour south of the Texas border, drug cartels killed twenty-one people, including four Mexican police officers. Their caravan included two dozen SUVs and was estimated to include over one hundred armed men. The Coahuila governor,

Miguel Ángel Riquelme Solís, said, "They go around through the U.S. part and they enter directly to the ranches in Coahuila towards Villa Union." But he later changed his story, "clarifying" that the cartels probably didn't enter the United States. Most people familiar with the incident—including me—believe he changed his story out of fear. The fact is these cartels don't respect the border at all. Cross-border crime is rampant.

It's not unusual for certain cartel vehicles to have their name and logo on the door. That's how corrupt and lawless life is in some parts of northern Mexico. In just the first ten months of 2019, there were 29,414 homicides in Mexico.

And our lack of security, lack of a wall, and lack of resolve only strengthens these cartels.

Most Americans haven't heard of the CJNG cartel, but many Mexican immigrants are all too familiar with this criminal organization. Cartel members follow many illegal aliens into the US and prey on their vulnerabilities, getting desperate immigrants to use drugs, sell drugs, launder money, and become involved with prostitution. Once involved, they threaten them with violence against them or their family, unless they expand their work for the cartel. Frighteningly, this and other cartels don't operate in big cities, where you might expect. They exploit rural communities across the country. Cartels are here, and their business is thriving.

The DOJ's Bureau of Justice Statistics report says that, even though the percentage of noncitizens in this country is less than 2 percent, in 2018, "Non-U.S. citizens accounted for 24% of all federal drug arrests and 25% of all federal property arrests, including 28% of all federal fraud arrests." In that same year, the number of federal arrests of Mexican citizens exceeded the number of federal arrests of US citizens.

CARTELS ARE TERRORIST ORGANIZATIONS

As of this writing, President Trump is considering classifying cartels as terrorist groups while trying to work with Mexico, convincing them to give US law enforcement a significant role in attacking these cartels. Based on what I've seen, they certainly meet every definition of terrorism. This designation would be a huge help to law enforcement, and it would also mean that anyone paying a cartel—for drugs or transport across the border—could be prosecuted for aiding a terrorist organization. Here are some pros and cons of the proposal.

The pros would be a more coordinated approach with a much larger US law enforcement participation—and along with this, more funding, more personnel, and better intelligence analysis. The terrorist designation can be effective.

Frankly, Mexico has failed to properly address the cartels for four decades or more. They operate with impunity in Mexico, and because of some corruption in Mexican law enforcement and military, the challenge is even greater. Please note that I said *some* are corrupt. There are certainly many dedicated Mexican law enforcement officers and military who serve honorably. Many have given their lives in the fight. Mexico simply doesn't have the expertise that the United States Department of Homeland Security or Department of Justice has.

The potential downside of a terrorist designation is that the Mexican government would almost certainly be offended, which could put their much-needed cooperation on the border in jeopardy. President Trump's pressure has led Mexico to do more than they have in decades to stem the tide of illegal crossings, and it's working. The terrorist designation may also embolden more Mexicans to come to our border and fraudulently claim asylum.

In my view, the United States should treat cartels as terrorist organizations but stop short of official designation. Let's use our investigative expertise, intelligence analysis, and prosecutorial skills to lead this attack and achieve the same results without the designation. We have proven we can be effective doing this. We did it in Panama with Manuel Noriega, in Mexico with El Chapo, and in Colombia with Mario Rendón Herrera and Carlos Lehder Rivas.

Here's one more aspect to consider regarding why it's so crucial to lead Mexico in the fight against cartels. If the violence isn't addressed, it's only a matter of time before those on the Left will shop for a federal judge to rule that Mexico should no longer be designated as a "safe third country." This would end the practice of returning those claiming asylum to Mexico. If this happens, the surge will quickly return at levels we've never seen. Cartels will use the ruling to sell their services to even more Central Americans.

A safer Mexico leads to a safer United States and a more secure border. Sadly, the Mexican government has done more to protect Americans than the Democrat leadership of Congress.

WHY AREN'T MORE CRIMES REPORTED?

Immigrant gangs, cartels, and petty criminals primarily victimize other immigrants. Why? Sanctuary city policies put offenders right back in their neighborhoods—so why would law-abiding immigrants stick their necks out? Many unlawful residents are afraid to go to law enforcement because of their immigration status, and this fear stems from the lies that many Democrats have spread about ICE. The fact is, illegal aliens who are victims of crime, or who help law enforcement convict criminals, can be eligible for legal status. Since assimilation is not promoted by Leftist leaders, these immigrants stay in a dangerous subculture.

These people are exploited by unethical employers and criminal gangs. It breaks my heart, because I've met victims of cartel violence. I've seen what gangs do to innocent people and their communities. But the fact that the Left lies about ICE and the Border Patrol—and local law enforcement—ticks me off, because it keeps these people in the shadows and prevents them from getting help.

Many of these immigrants arrive in this country with a gripping fear of law enforcement because of police corruption in their home country. They don't realize that the United States has the most compassionate and ethical law enforcement on the planet. And why would they? Some Democrats proclaim that our officers are Nazis. These politicians are directly responsible for rising crime at the hands of illegal alien criminals—and for the suffering in these communities.

FOREIGN NATIONALS IN PRISON

The Department of Justice and Department of Homeland Security released a "Quarterly Alien Incarceration Report" on June 7, 2018. A Department of Justice news release about the report said that "more than one-in-five of all persons in Bureau of Prisons custody were known or suspected aliens, and 93 percent of confirmed aliens in DOJ custody were in the United States unlawfully."

It went on to say, "Approximately 16,233 aliens in USMS [US Marshals Service] custody required housing in state, local, and private facilities, which cost $1,458,372.72 a day." That's nearly $1.5 million—every single day, seven days a week—totaling over $500 million per year.

It further states, "As reported by the Texas Department of Public Safety (DPS), 251,000 criminal aliens have been booked into local Texas jails between June 1, 2011 and April 30, 2018, according to DHS status indicators. These criminal aliens were charged with:

- More than 663,000 criminal offenses;
- 1,351 homicides;
- 7,156 sexual assaults;
- 9,938 weapons charges;
- 79,049 assaults;
- 18,685 burglaries;
- 79,900 drug charges;
- 815 kidnappings;
- 44,882 thefts;
- 4,292 robberies."

When you read these numbers, pause and consider what they represent. Not only is there a huge number of criminal aliens in custody. Their crimes affect hundreds of thousands of innocent human beings every year.

ICE LOOKS FOR CRIMINALS

Operation Safe Neighborhoods was a program we developed when I was head of investigations in San Antonio. One of my supervisors at the time, Matthew Albence, currently the acting director of ICE, came up with a concept of having dedicated operations focused on illegal alien criminals. These operations were very successful and took hundreds of criminals off the streets. When I went to head-quarters and became the assistant director for enforcement, in charge of enforcement operations within the interior United States, we built on that experience and launched Operation Cross Check across all twenty-four field offices nationwide. ICE and INS always prioritized criminals, but this concept was for a nationwide surge operation over a short time period to create immediate impact and make those communities measurably safer.

We arrested thousands upon thousands of criminal aliens. In one weeklong nationwide operation, we arrested over two thousand illegal aliens who were a danger to those communities. ICE arrested 137,000 criminal aliens in 2018. In ten years, over 1 million criminals are no longer in our communities—and this is just the number arrested by ICE. Add in the Border Patrol, FBI, and state and local law enforcement, and we're talking about up to 10 million in the past decade. If you think we have a crime problem now, imagine our nation with millions more criminals roaming the streets.

A REPEAT OFFENDER NAMED ALIAS

If an illegal alien is caught by Border Patrol, the agent asks for the person's name and other pertinent information. What most people in this country don't realize is that the name given might not be their real name. This is especially true for those who are hiding a criminal record, or those who've been deported before—perhaps dozens of times—under false names.

Of course, our federal agents are well trained and have pretty accurate bullshit detectors. I've personally arrested illegal aliens, run their fingerprints, and matched twenty aliases. Not until the past decade did we start fingerprinting everyone detained at the border. Back in the day, we didn't take fingerprints unless we were going to prosecute them. When I was on the Border Patrol Prosecution Unit back in 1987, I'd file the case with the US attorney's office, then run his fingerprints. Today, they simply upload the prints to the computer database. Back then, we had to go through files of index cards with fingerprints and manually look for a match. Yes, really.

In addition to getting an accurate name, determining their real country of origin is tricky. Many of those from Central America claim to be from Mexico, because they've been coached. They knew they'd be released either into the United States or simply across the border to Mexico—where they could easily try to reenter. If they admit to being Honduran or Guatemalan, they might be flown back to their home country on the next removal flight. And who wants to make that long, dangerous journey again? In my early days, I don't know how many times I'd take someone claiming to be Mexican to the port of entry and turn him over to the Mexican officials. Within a few hours, or the next day, the Mexican customs office would return the person to us because he was not a citizen of their country. Of course, many Mexican authorities had their own way of interrogating someone, which is to say they were nowhere near as humane.

We learned to ask certain questions in a certain way because of slight variations in the Spanish language. Ask a question with certain terminology and their answer would, for example, tell you they were really from Honduras. We had ten questions, and a map.

"Where are you from?"

"Mexico."

"What town?"

"Guadalajara."

"What's the closest town to the north?"

That question would bust many of them. The point is, law enforcement is difficult enough with a porous border and lack of verifiable identification. Even with today's technology, all the bad guys will still lie about their identity, and fingerprint records aren't perfect. However, with portable fingerprint scanners and almost instant results, it's certainly a lot easier today than it was when I wore the green uniform. Identification is paramount, and that is why federal agencies are starting to use DNA in a pilot program to confirm "family units" are actually related. We know that many are not.

A quick note as I reminisce about my time in the Border Patrol. There were no computers. There were no cell phones. I processed paperwork on the hood of my vehicle, and you had to press the pen down hard to go through four sets of carbon paper. When we created a prosecution report, we had to find a workable typewriter and a barrel of Wite-Out. Man, I'm old.

CRIME AND PUNISHMENT

What you legalize, or don't enforce, you get more of. What you criminalize, or enforce, you get less of. It's common sense.

Look at San Francisco. In particular, look down at their streets. They've either legalized or don't enforce laws against panhandling, vagrancy, drug use, "petty" theft, and public defecation—and the city is swimming in it all. San Francisco also happens to be a sanctuary jurisdiction, which has led to a growing illegal alien population.

In later 2019, New York governor Andrew Cuomo signed the Green Light law, which offers driver's licenses for illegal aliens. This legislation disgusts me. The law specifically prohibits the state from sharing information with federal law enforcement. In other words, New York can give licenses to those who came to, or stayed in, this country in violation of our laws, but the identities of these people can't be shared with DHS or ICE. Federal law is clear: It's a crime to "conceal, harbor or shield from detection an individual living illegally in the United States." It's also a federal crime to create a policy that prevents government employees from sharing information with ICE. Thankfully, the DOJ is looking into this legislation that seems to run counter to federal law.

If you needed clear evidence that Leftist legislators care more about illegal aliens than law-abiding citizens, there's your proof.

On December 6, 2019, a Saudi terrorist, who was enrolled in pilot training at Florida's Naval Air Station Pensacola, shot and killed several Americans in the classroom. As he carried out the attack, his fellow countrymen stood by and recorded video of the shooting. It was later learned that a few days before the murders, the shooter and three of his friends held a dinner party where they watched videos of mass shootings. These terrorists didn't simply come to the US as tourists—they went through high-level security screenings to enroll at a military training facility, and they attended for many months. If the military couldn't spot murderers inside our training academy, why are politicians so confident about the absolute strangers crossing our border every day?

Congress's job is to protect American citizens. Unless we enforce our laws, we will see more lawlessness.

TOUGH COOKIES

At that same June 2017 event in New York where the president addressed officers conducting the massive anti-gang operation, he also said this in his speech: "I especially want to thank ICE director Tom Homan, who has done an incredible job in just a short period of time. Tom is determined to rid our nation of cartels and criminals who are preying on our citizens. And I can only say to Tom: Keep up the great work. He's a tough guy. He's a tough cookie. Somebody said the other day, they saw him on television, and said, 'He looks very nasty, he looks very mean.' I said, 'That's what I'm looking for. That's exactly what I was looking for.'"

When it comes to needless crime, when it comes to protecting human beings from animals, the men and women of law enforcement are "mean." That's exactly what we need.

NINE

BUILD THOSE WALLS

565,581 San Diego sector apprehensions in 1992, and 26,086
in 2017—before and after a wall was built there.
—US Customs and Border Patrol report

In four Customs and Border Protection sectors where physical
barriers have been expanded—El Paso, Yuma, Tucson, and San
Diego—illegal traffic has dropped by at least 90%.
—BorderFacts.com

As Border Patrol agent in Southern California, I "dragged" dirt roads many, many times. We'd take an old tractor tire, cut it in half like a bagel, and then drag it cut side down along the endless miles of dirt roads near the border. No, we weren't obsessive about smooth roads. We needed to be able to spot fresh tracks of those crossing north.

The other half of our dusty work was "cutting sign"—driving slowly over the fresh roads and looking for signs of illegal aliens. Of course, the smugglers would try to cover their tracks using tree branches to sweep the trail behind them. But an experienced agent could spot one of these "brush outs" from the seat of his truck. And in Campo, California, we had some of the best trackers in the business.

The East-West Road was a long, dirt road close to the barbed-wire fence along the border. I must have dragged that route hundreds of times. Because we were in a mountainous region, we had less foot traffic than in San Ysidro, but this was a main entry point for dope carriers, who knew we had fewer agents in the area. At the time, all agents carried a Ruger Security-Six—a six-shot revolver. Certainly not a match for some of the weapons the bad guys used.

During one midnight shift, on September 26, 1986, I was patrolling alone at two a.m. when dispatch called out a drive-through sensor near Jacumba, California. Another agent radioed that he was close and on his way, and I also headed to the area. Within a few minutes he reported that he saw the vehicle heading north from the trigger zone and said he would stop it once it went onto the highway. The agent was a seasoned veteran and asked me and another unit to get to the scene as soon as we could. I drove as quickly as possible, with emergency lights flashing, and soon saw that he successfully pulled over the vehicle—a large, brown, utility-type pickup with compartments on the side and in the back, like a plumber or electrician might use. The agent already had a male subject out of the truck and in handcuffs. I placed the subject in the back of my Ram Charger. As I returned, another agent arrived, and we opened a storage area along the side of the truck. The compartment was crammed full of packages of white powder. Cocaine. As we continued, every chamber contained the same cargo.

Exhilaration turned to fear in an instant. The arresting agent yelled at us to watch for traffic and be prepared to encounter an armed escort vehicle. He also called dispatch for any and all available law enforcement to get to the area—and fast. We knew that cargo this valuable was always followed by a crew of heavily armed escorts. I grabbed the shotgun from the cab of my pickup, stood at the front of my truck, and carefully watched every vehicle as it approached—and slowly passed by. Within about fifteen minutes, plenty of good guys with guns had arrived, and the secluded section of highways was lit up like Las Vegas.

During trial we learned that there was indeed an escort car. They were waiting just down the highway at the next exit. When the truck didn't show up, they drove back toward us. Seeing the flashing lights and army of armed law enforcement, they kept on driving. Several months later, after a successful trial, the three of us received awards from the head of DEA and the sector chief of the Border Patrol in recognition of what was, at the time, the biggest drug bust in Border Patrol history: 1,284 pounds of cocaine.

Imagine if the senior agent hadn't caught the smuggler so quickly, or if he had pulled him over near the armed escort. What if I, or the third agent, had arrived a few minutes later—or if local law enforcement hadn't joined us? The story would have had a very different ending. I pondered that scenario for many weeks.

But here's another question to consider. What if, instead of a flimsy, barbed-wire fence along the border, there was a big, beautiful wall—a border barrier made of steel?

When I attended the International Association of Chiefs of Police convention in San Diego two years ago, I drove my rental car to Campo to reminisce about the days I had spent there more than thirty years before. Much looked and felt the same. But the biggest change was a tall steel fence that stood along the border. *I wish we had that in 1986*, I thought. No trucks will be driving across this section of the border anymore.

BARRIERS AND BORDERS

I remember watching then candidate Trump give a speech in Arizona in 2016. As someone who'd been on the front lines of the border crisis for thirty years, I paid attention to every word.

Everything he said about illegal immigration was right on target. I wondered how a billionaire from New York could know so much about the Southwest border. He talked about the wall. In San Diego, back in the early eighties, we arrested thousands of migrants a night. Many would line up on the soccer field just south of the border. As soon as the sun went down, they rushed the border. It was a free-for-all. Then something changed. San Diego finally built its first section of barrier, and the impact was immediate. Just this year, I spoke with the chief patrol agent, and he confirmed that the fencing still helps them maintain a high degree of operational control. The numbers dropped drastically, and the human traffic moved east toward El Centro, Campo, and Yuma.

Barriers are effective. They reduce illegal immigration and drug smuggling. Walls have never been about stopping people; they're about slowing people down and giving the Border Patrol time to respond. Effective barriers stop vehicles and funnel people to areas where limited security resources make the greatest impact.

THIRTY-FOOT WALL, FORTY-FOOT LADDER

Critics of the border wall pretend to want measures that work. They argue, "If we build a thirty-foot wall, they will bring a forty-foot ladder." Sure, any wall can be climbed. But it takes a lot of effort to get over a well-built one. And it takes a lot longer to get a ladder and scale a wall than it does to stroll across a road.

"See? They can cut through the wall!" The point isn't that a wall can't be cut. Any barrier will slow people down. And consider this: The people trying to cut the wall are not families; they are drug smugglers and human traffickers. Criminals hate walls.

"But all the walls are just replacement sections!" Yeah, I've heard this one, too. The media's been shouting, "You're not building a new wall; you're just replacing old walls." When it came time to start construction, the experts—most importantly the Border Patrol—recommended the most crucial areas where the new wall designs should be built. Unsurprisingly, many of these high-traffic areas happen to have outdated or broken-down barriers. Every mile of wall being built isn't a "new" wall in a new area—yet. But it is a new, more effective wall in the most trafficked area as identified by the experts on the ground. If the front door on your house doesn't shut and lock, you'd replace the door before you put new bars on the windows, wouldn't you?

"Experts say a wall is ineffective." I'd like to meet those "experts." I promise you one thing: They never wore a green uniform. They never stood post on our southern border, and they never arrested a criminal alien, drug smuggler, or human trafficker. Let's just say I know hundreds of people who've served on our southern border, and we all agree that walls work.

DESIGNING DETERRENTS

In the Rio Grande Valley, solid concrete walls are designed to double as flood control. But most of the wall will be made of steel posts, called bollards. This design was favored by Border Patrol agents because we need to be able to see what, and who, is on the other side of the barrier. In some cases, the steel pillars will be filled with concrete. Another advantage of these steel walls is they can be quickly repaired if breached or damaged. Instead of having to replace entire sections of wall, the individual bollards are designed to be replaced quickly and efficiently.

Prototypes were put through a series of tests conducted by SWAT teams and various military specialists. "Give it your best shot," they were told. "Can you climb over it? Drill through it? Dig under it?" The experts who tried to beat the prototypes found problems and strengths with each design. They identified the positive features in each of the prototypes and worked to create the best model. A height of thirty feet was determined to be optimal, because most people become very uncomfortable that far off the ground. Again, walls are deterrents.

POLITICAL WALLS

Regardless of the current political climate, most Democrats have supported border barriers in the past. One of the earliest, real-deal walls was constructed between San Diego and Tijuana, and it was constructed during the Clinton administration.

In 2005, Senator Barack Obama said, "We are a generous and welcoming people here in the United States. But those who enter the country illegally and those who employ them disrespect the rule of law and they are showing disregard for those who are following the law. We simply cannot allow people to pour into the United States undetected, undocumented, unchecked, and circumventing the line of people who are waiting patiently, diligently, and lawfully to become immigrants into this country."

During the George W. Bush administration, the Secure Fence Act of 2006, which included $1.4 billion for seven hundred miles of fence on the southern border, was signed into law after then senators Barack Obama and Hillary Clinton voted for it, along with Senator Chuck Schumer. "The bill before us will certainly do some good. It will authorize some badly needed funding for better fences and better security along our borders, and that should help stem some of the tide of illegal immigration in this country," Senator Obama said about the legislation.

In 2011, President Obama bragged that under his leadership, "We have strengthened border security beyond what many believed was possible. We now have more boots on the ground on the southwest border than at any time in our history. The Border Patrol has twenty thousand agents, more than twice as many as there were in 2004, a build-up that began under President Bush and that we have continued." Wow. Can you imagine Nancy Pelosi or any 2020 Democrat presidential candidate bragging about "boots on the ground" of the border or the success of the Secure Fence Act?

"I voted numerous times when I was a senator to spend money to build a barrier to try to prevent illegal immigrants from coming in." Who said that? Hillary Clinton in November 2015.

Today, we get meaningless doublespeak from most of the Left. For example, recently Speaker Pelosi said, "The fact is we all agree we need to secure our borders while honoring our values." Okay, pause a second. What the heck does that mean? She went on to say, "We can build the infrastructure and roads at our ports of entry. We can install new technology to scan cars and trucks for drugs coming into our nation. We can hire the personnel we need to facilitate trade and immigration at the border. We can fund more innovation to detect unauthorized crossings." Again, she uses lots of security-related words, but they add up to nothing.

Technology is important. Staffing is critical. But you can't drive a truck full of drugs—or a tractor-trailer full of people—over a wall.

The Democrat leadership keeps saying they want to invest at the ports of entry because "that's where most of the illegal drugs come into the country." This is a deceptive argument, meant to discredit the effectiveness of physical barriers. Yes, most of the drugs are seized at a port because every car is stopped and every driver is interviewed. Not every vehicle is searched, but the interview and observation can lead to a search. When you have this level of screening, chances are you'll be more successful at seizing contraband. However, more drugs seized at a port does not mean more drugs come through a port. We don't know what we don't know. If someone wants to smuggle large amounts of cocaine into the US, would they go through a port where they know they'll be stopped and questioned, or would they enter illegally, between the ports, where there isn't a wall?

As soon as President Trump was elected, many Democrats forgot about real border security. Instead of touting their efforts to bring law and order to the crisis, they called those same intentions racist and somehow at odds with American values. They accused the president of being obsessed with a "vanity project." But in doing so, Leftists actually insulted the tens of millions of citizens who see the obvious need for a secure border, and they insult the tens of thousands of law enforcement officers who know that walls work. I've witnessed it personally. The president listens to the real experts, which is all too rare in my experience. With the current strategy for more border walls, the Border Patrol will receive exactly what they want and where they want it. This isn't the president's wall; it is America's wall. Why is it so hard to understand that the president's success on this issue is America's success? I have never seen anything like it in my career. Half of Congress wants to see this president's agenda fail, even if it risks America's safety and our sovereignty. It doesn't matter if you're a Republican, Democrat, independent, or even a socialist; your number one responsibility as our elected official is to protect the citizens of our country. There is no downside to fewer drugs coming across our border, less illegal immigration, and less money funding the criminal cartels. Those elected to Congress should love this country more than they hate their political rivals.

MORE WALLS, FEWER PROBLEMS

As more miles of modern walls are built, fewer Border Patrol agents are put at risk. As fewer criminals enter, fewer citizens are at risk. As fewer illegal aliens cross, fewer resources are needed to feed and care for them. As drug smugglers face real barriers, fewer drugs enter the US. As human traffickers are stopped, fewer women and children are exploited. Walls save money, but more importantly, they save lives.

When I was a Border Patrol agent in California, the Campo area had a lot of drug smuggling via car and truck across the border. They simply cut the old wire fencing and drove right in. Just south of the border was a little Mexican village of about thirty humble homes. We used to bring them clothes and food when we could. When we were looking for smugglers, I'd yell across the border, "Hey, someone just drove through. Can you tell me what the car looks like?" Very often, they'd give me a description of the vehicle. They didn't want criminals in their community any more than you or I would. A few years ago, I drove around the area and went there to see if the village was still there. I couldn't tell you if it was. All I saw was a huge wall.

PAYING FOR THE WALL

I've worked in law enforcement during six presidential administrations. Each one played a budget game with the border: a little money here, a little fence there. "Where do you need it the most? Okay. We'll give you twenty miles of fence, here, in exchange for concessions on these other issues." Both sides were okay with this arrangement, until candidate Donald Trump promised to build a wall across the entire southwest border. He asked the question my colleagues and I had asked for decades: Why are we putting Band-Aids on the border when we can actually have an effective wall?

That question, and his promise, sure got the country riled up. And open-borders advocates argued that walls didn't work. When that view was shown to be idiotic, they pretended to care about the price tag.

A $5 billion wall will pay for itself in a decade. I'm not a budget guy, but the math is so simple. Let's crunch some numbers.

The current annual budget to provide medical care in detention is $500 million. If we cut that by just 50 percent, that's $250 million saved each year, which pays for the wall in twenty years. As they say on TV infomercials, "But wait, there's more!" ICE spends about $2 billion per year on detention. Cut the number in half, and put $1 billion toward the wall—paid in five years.

According to the Federation for American Immigration Reform, the total cost of illegal immigration totals $116 billion—per year. Using a figure of 12.5 million illegal aliens currently in this country, they break down the numbers this way:

Federal education: $1.6 billion
Federal medical costs: $17.1 billion
Federal justice expenditures: $13.1 billion
Federal welfare programs: $5.8 billion
Total federal expenditures: $45.8 billion
State educational expenditures: $44.4 billion
State medical expenditures: $12.1 billion
State administration of justice expenditures: $10.8 billion
State welfare expenditures: $2.9 billion
State and local expenditures: $88 billion
Total cost to state and federal government: $133.8 billion

When you add in the estimated taxes illegal aliens pay back into the state and federal budgets ($18 billion), the net cost to our country totals $116 billion. Skeptical? Good. We should always have a healthy skepticism about claims from either side of the debate. So let's say these estimated costs are exaggerated—even doubled. That's still $58 billion per year. What if these numbers are so blatantly bloated that they must have multiplied them by ten—no, *twenty*. One-twentieth of their estimate is $5.8 billion.

It's not rocket science. When you start adding up all the direct and indirect costs involved in reduced employment for citizens, identity theft, food, housing, medical care, social programs, courts, education, lost tax revenue, Border Patrol budgets, and ICE budgets, anyone can see that a $5 billion investment in a real wall will pay for itself. If more jobs were filled with US citizens and legal immigrants, tax revenues would certainly go up—along with wages.

WALL OR REVOLVING DOOR?

Without a wall, our border is a revolving door for bad guys. Gang members and those with criminal records don't usually drive through legal ports of entry, because they know our database continues to improve.

One particular arrest from my career comes to mind. The man was missing several fingers on his right hand. He told me he'd lost them in a farming accident. I arrested him around nine o'clock in the morning on the east side of the port of entry, processed him—an experienced agent could process an illegal alien in just twenty minutes—and drove him back to the border. A couple hours later, I arrested him coming over the west side of the port of entry. We processed him again. We sent him back. That afternoon, a sensor went off in an area outside my patrol, but the other agent was busy. As I drove up to the man, he turned to me and started laughing. By now, we had a pretty good routine, and I processed him in record time.

Later that afternoon, an agent walked into the office with an arrestee. "Did you just arrest him?" I asked.

"Yeah, do you know this guy?"

"You could say that. I arrested him three times today."

On the surface, this might sound like a funny story. The problem is, this happens every day on sections of our border that do not have a wall. When you hear yet another horrible news report about violence committed by an illegal alien who was "previously deported six times," think about the need for a border wall.

As I've said, walls are not a 100 percent solution, but they slow down 100 percent of the people who try to cross our border. The new wall design also incorporates technology that alerts the Border Patrol when someone tries to drill, dig, or climb. With our Border Patrol agents spending more time babysitting—literally taking care of young, unaccompanied kids—we need a wall more than ever. If human smuggling becomes more difficult, fewer immigrants will partner with criminal cartels, which means fewer cases of abuse.

WHAT SHOULD BE DONE?

Obviously, we need to build the wall—across much of the entire southern border. Where a traditional concept of a "wall" isn't practical, use technology to create barriers and alerts. There are sections of the border where the landscape itself provides a barrier, such as where there are steep cliffs. But we must stop accepting excuses and insist on sincere efforts to secure the border.

What's stalling the wall? Congress will not fully fund it. Why haven't they allocated the money? Because too many voters still believe the misleading talking points of the Left. Hopefully I've discredited their ignorant arguments, and hopefully you feel emboldened in your support for the wall.

In the 2020 election, we can send a clear message to Congress by firing those who play games with the border and, as a result, enable human suffering on a scale you can't imagine.

Sometimes the simplest fixes are the best fixes. Walls work. You may have one around your yard. Many politicians do.

TEN

ARE BORDERS RACIST?

0

—The number of convictions for cases of violation of human rights by ICE or Border Patrol agents based on race

In a July 2019 hearing before Congress, Illinois Democrat Jesús García decided to grill me on the topic of zero tolerance. If you missed this exchange, let me break it down for you.

"Mr. Homan," he began. "Do you understand that the consequences of separation of many children will be lifelong trauma and carried across generations?"

Illegal immigration and other serious crimes do result in family separation and trauma—I've seen it firsthand on countless occasions and know more about the issues than Jesús García ever will. But then Representative García took a hard left turn from the issue and launched into accusations of racism.

"Have we not learned from the internment of Japanese Americans?"

Excuse me, but what the hell does enforcing our laws at the border have to do with rounding up those of Japanese descent during World War II?

Then he got personal.

"Mr. Homan, I'm a father. Do you have children? How can you possibly allow this to happen under your watch? Do you not care? *Is it because these children don't look like children that are around you?* I don't get it. *Have you ever held a deceased child in your arms?*"

I was enraged. Yes, his stupidity and ignorance were shocking. *But was this politician accusing me of not caring about these children because they don't look like me?* He doesn't know me. He hasn't seen what I have seen throughout my career. He wasn't there when my colleagues and I comforted a young female migrant who had been repeatedly raped before crossing in the US. He wasn't there when we entered a load house and found women who were sex slaves to the smugglers. He wasn't there when I couldn't sleep for several days after seeing that dead five-year-old lying in the back of a trailer in Victoria, Texas. He wasn't there when I attended funerals and tried to console the spouses and children of Border Patrol agents and special agents who died while serving their nation. He hasn't seen the investigations and operations that I led throughout my career, which undoubtedly saved thousands of migrants' lives.

I served my nation and sacrificed—and my family also sacrificed. For some politician to ignore all this and characterize me as racist was, truly, the worst thing anyone has ever said to me in my lifetime. As a man, I wanted to fight, but as a career law enforcement officer and law-abiding citizen, I defended myself with the truth, loudly and clearly.

I quickly responded, "Yes, I held a five-year-old boy in my arms in the back of a tractor trailer. I knelt down beside him and said a prayer for him, because I knew what the last thirty minutes of his life were like. And I had a five-year-old son at the time. What I've been trying to do my thirty-four years serving my nation is to save lives, so for you to sit there and insult my integrity and my love for my country and for children—that's why this whole thing needs to be fixed. You're a member of Congress. Fix it!"

If politicians spent as much time working on solutions as they do preparing sound bites and "gotcha" questions for their donors, we might actually make some progress. But this is what we're up against. They don't care about the underlying causes of the border crisis, because their policies and inaction are the cause. Instead of facing the problem head-on and apologizing to citizens, they attack me, the president, and the men and women of law enforcement.

THEIR ONLY WEAPON

In September 2019, Chicago Mayor Lori Lightfoot declared that the city—including its police—would not assist ICE. "We will never, ever succumb to the racist, xenophobic rhetoric of ICE. We will continue to ban ICE from having access to any CPD databases. We'll not allow any CPD officer to cooperate with anything related to ICE and its immigration raids."

This "sanctuary city" mayor basically called ICE agents and leadership racists. Civil debate is over in Chicago and most big cities in this country. Crime statistics and new policy ideas to protect citizens are off the table. The *r*-word is their only weapon, and they use it without even thinking.

Remember, when the Left attacks law enforcement as "racist," they're also accusing you. I'm not racist. In fact, I've met many people in my life from all walks of life, and I've actually met very few people who I thought were racist. Accusing people of prejudice and hate is the last gasp of people with no argument. Ignore them, unless they can show evidence of actual racism.

As a cop, I arrested people who broke the law. As Border Patrol agents, we arrested people who broke the law. More than half the agents are Hispanic, by the way. And ICE doesn't arrest people based on race; ICE arrests people who are in the country illegally—no matter their race or country of origin. Last year, ICE arrested people from 130 different countries. Most of these illegal aliens have had their day in court and received an order from a judge to leave. Are these judges also racist? I don't remember any of this screaming during previous presidential administrations. As soon as candidate Trump started talking about the border, the racist cheerleaders came onto the field.

In 2018, Brooklyn Democrat representative Yvette Clarke said in a speech outside New York ICE offices, "We're standing in front of a building that has become the headquarters for the Gestapo of the United States of America." You've also heard AOC accuse ICE of running "concentration camps." I've been called a racist, and protesters have stood outside my home yelling "Nazi!" It's a sad day in America when we're called racist simply for enforcing the law.

In another congressional testimony in 2019, I asked the representatives a simple question: "If ICE agents are racist for enforcing the laws that Congress enacts, what does that make you—who wrote and passed the laws, and who refuse to propose new legislation?" Does this make them racists? Certainly not, and neither are the law enforcement officers who follow the rules they enacted.

Where was all this "racist" hysteria in 2012, under the Obama administration, when ICE arrested and removed over 409,000 illegal aliens from the country? This is almost twice as many as ICE removed last year under President Trump. Where was this hateful rhetoric in 2014 and 2015 under the previous administration when we increased family detention by 3,000 percent, going from one hundred family beds to more than three thousand family beds. Where was the fake outrage when, at one point during the Obama administration, only about 59 percent of the people we removed were convicted criminals? Under President Trump, the percentage of ICE arrests involving criminals is almost 89 percent.

In other congressional testimony, on September 11, 2019, Congresswoman Debbie Wasserman Schultz began her time at the microphone demanding that my opening statement be stricken from the record. "I think it's important to really make sure that the jingoistic, bigoted testimony of Mr. Homan is called out as nearly completely untrue, as being an outrage, and as a former official directing the Immigration and Customs Enforcement agency, he should know better," she said.

"What did I say that was inaccurate?" I shot back.

"I just think it's important that it's not accepted as accurate testimony," she replied.

I waited until my next opportunity to speak, and said, "If I can respond to the earlier remark from Wasserman Schultz, I've forgotten more about this issue than you'll ever know. So, if you say my testimony is inaccurate, it's wrong. Everything I said here is accurate. Bottom line: if you want to go toe to toe, I'm here. I'm here on my own time to speak to the American people about what's false and what's fact."

"I'm happy to go toe to toe with you, Mr. Homan, I'm happy to do that any day."

"Then you got to let me respond to your question rather than dropping a bomb and running away," I asserted, and then continued. "ICE doesn't put their heart on a shelf when they wear the badge and gun and all of a sudden don't care about humanity. It's ridiculous. It's a ridiculous false narrative, and I'm going to be here 'til the day I die defending the men and women of the Border Patrol and ICE who put it on the line defending this country."

IGNORANT AND EVIL

I've spent the majority of my life serving my nation and have been involved in many dangerous situations. I don't consider myself a milquetoast, but I will share this with you: No matter how tough someone is, no matter how thick their skin, no matter how right they think they are, it still hurts to be compared to the Nazis, who were the most notorious, evil, and vicious group of people in modern history. To actually compare what our law enforcement officers do every day to the heinous atrocities of the Holocaust is disgusting on every level. It's disrespectful to the victims of the Holocaust, and to the thousands of American soldiers who fought in World War II. Anyone who attempts to correlate enforcement of immigration law to the Holocaust is not worthy of our attention— let alone a seat in elected office. Shame on them.

Racism is ignorant and evil. It's also a very emotional issue, and rightly so. Racism involves judging people based on their race, not their character, and everyone knows it's wrong. Accusing people of racism incites hatred and violence. Even if the accusation is a slanderous lie, some people will believe it.

In August 2019, multiple gunshots were fired at a San Antonio ICE office. The Enforcement and Removal Operations field office director said, "Political rhetoric and misinformation that various politicians, media outlets, and activist groups recklessly disseminate to the American people regarding the ICE mission only serve to further encourage these violent acts." The overwhelming amount of hateful rhetoric comes from the Left. And it puts our law enforcement in danger. And while they're focusing on this false narrative, the real issues aren't being discussed.

In September 2019, a man attacked an ICE detention facility in Washington State with a firearm and tried to blow up a propane tank. The man previously wrote a rambling manifesto that declared, "It's time to take action against the forces of evil" and "highly profitable detention/concentration camps." Where did he hear that comparison? Maybe from Congressperson Alexandria Ocasio-Cortez.

The head of the US Immigration and Customs Enforcement's Office of Professional Responsibility said, "This could have resulted in the mass murder of staff and detainees housed at the facility, had he been successful at setting the tank ablaze." If there's anything we need to come together on quickly, it is to stop the hateful rhetoric because it's only a matter of time before an ICE agent gets killed, a family member gets hurt, or a facility is murderously attacked. Charges of racism have done nothing but stir up hate against law enforcement officers.

The Department of Homeland Security Office for Civil Rights and Civil Liberties Antidiscrimination Group engages in policy work to ensure equitable treatment of individuals and guard against discrimination based on race, color, national origin, disability, sex, and age. The number of complaints filed for possible "discrimination/profiling" have totaled only two hundred in the thirteen-year period from 2004 to 2016—even though DHS processes hundreds of thousands of people every year. I'm not aware of one substantiated case of a violation of human rights by ICE or Border Patrol based on race. There are dozens of agencies and organizations dedicated—even obsessed with—making sure ICE doesn't take any action that might be deemed racist. If they can't find anything, maybe there's nothing to be found.

COMPASSION AND CRIME

Just for a few minutes, let's play the Democrats' advocate and examine their point of view. For the record, I hate looking at any issue through the lens of race, but we need to show that their arguments don't make sense. Focusing on one particular example, if you really cared about Hispanic immigrants—legal and illegal—you would want as little crime as possible in neighborhoods that happen to be primarily populated by Hispanics. Yet policies like "catch and release" and sanctuary cities only increase the amount of crime and chaos in these communities. If you cared about the people who live in these areas (Hispanics, in this particular exercise), why would you release convicted felons back into their neighborhood instead of turning them over to ICE?

Politicians who promote open borders and sanctuary jurisdictions and talk about compassion for immigrant communities are hypocrites because their policies actually hurt immigrants. These policies cause division, not only between law enforcement and the community, but inside the community.

I'll be blunt. Politicians who promise free stuff for illegal aliens are pandering based on race. Democrats who won't turn illegal alien felons over to ICE don't advocate for that stance with US citizens. Justice must be blind. The alternative is . . . racist.

In October 2019, Rashida Tlaib, Democrat representative from Michigan, met with the Detroit chief of police to tour the department's new facial recognition technology. "Analysts need to be African Americans, not people that are not," Tlaib demanded. "It's true. I think non–African Americans think African Americans all look the same!"

The police chief, who happens to be black, immediately disagreed, saying, "I trust people who are trained, regardless of race, regardless of gender." Which one of these people sounds more racist to you?

In 2018, Barack Obama had a lot to say about President Trump's decision to move fifteen thousand troops to the southern border.

It was an election year, after all. "We have seen repeated attempts to divide us with rhetoric designed to make us angry and make us fearful. It's designed to exploit our history of racial and ethnic and religious division that pits us against one another, to make us believe that somehow order will be restored if it weren't just for those folks who don't look like we look." There's that accusation again, that fair-minded Americans can't want a secure border—the motivation must be racism. Chicago congressman García also accused me of racism "because these children don't look like children that are around you." Honestly, I don't know why the Democrats are so obsessed with race. But such is our political environment.

Don't forget, when the Left attacks law enforcement as "racist," they are not only attacking the law, they are ultimately attacking those who simply want respect for our laws. In other words, when they slander me, they're also trying to slander you. If you believe in the rule of law, if you believe a judge's deportation order should be carried out, if you believe in this nation's sovereignty and the right to secure our border, does that make you a racist? According to the Left, it does.

They claim immigration is all about race and caring for the poor. In reality, it's a brutal campaign to seize power. They will use any weapon at their disposal. Ignore the mob and their tactics. The desire for a secure border, a wall, and a transparent legal framework is not racist—it's common sense and compassionate.

ELEVEN

ZERO TOLERANCE AND THE FALLACY OF "FAMILY SEPARATION"

14,000 unaccompanied immigrant children
have been placed in U.S. custody.
—HEALTH AND HUMAN SERVICES (HHS) REPORT, NOVEMBER 2018

During the Obama administration, I was the executive associate director of ICE—third in command of the agency, overseeing interior enforcement operations for immigration. Jeh Johnson was the secretary of Homeland Security, and we always had a stellar professional relationship. I consider him a friend today, and I have said many times that I respect him greatly. Of course, we had many discussions about immigration. He asked for my recommendations to fix problems, and he did the same with our other colleagues. In the end, Johnson implemented some and disagreed with others. But he cared about the border and sought the best ideas. He didn't always like or agree with what I said, but he told me he wanted to hear my perspective. At the very least, if he decided against me, he wanted to know what the upside and downside were. He sincerely wanted all ideas and options discussed.

I know it seems like ancient history, but at the time, the Obama administration was very concerned about reducing illegal immigration, especially in 2014 and 2015. At one meeting in the White House situation room, one of President Obama's immigration advisors suggested that ICE needed to deport children who arrived here unaccompanied and were ordered by a judge to be removed. I looked at her in disbelief, took a deep breath, and offered the following reply: "Do you want me to take a minor child out of their home? That's not something we do or have ever done, and I'm not comfortable doing it. Why not put the entire family in proceedings if they're all in violation of a judge's order—or wait 'til the child is eighteen and assess their criminal record? Do you realize what you're asking us to do?"

The room got quiet for a moment and the response was, yes, we know exactly what we're asking to be done.

While I scribbled notes, I said, "Let me think of some options here and get back to you." A few weeks later, my deputy had a similar conversation with the same staff, and the same suggestion was made again. He told them that not only was the proposal a logistical nightmare, but it would put people in danger and create terrible public perception of the administration. I thought the idea was zero tolerance on steroids—and idiotic. The illegal alien parent gets to stay because they haven't been arrested yet or may not have a final order issued by a judge, but since we have a final order on the child, we arrest and remove only the child?

Obviously, the Obama administration never enacted that policy because we pushed back, but it shows you how big the problem was and how concerned they were about chaotic conditions on the border. Trust me, there were even worse ideas floated in our meetings. I'd also like to point out that the "heartless" Tom Homan stood up to the Obama administration and said no.

THE REALITY OF FAMILY SEPARATION

As a police officer in New York, I took people into custody for various crimes. One arrest stands out. I once had to arrest a father for domestic violence against his wife, who'd been repeatedly brutalized. His young daughter begged me not to take him to jail. My heart was torn by her tears, but in order to protect her and her mother I had no choice. As sad as it was, he needed to be held accountable for what he did. In his cell, this father was separated from his family—just like every inmate in every jail and prison in the world. Sometimes enforcing the law can be unspeakably sad. Law enforcement officers deal with tragic and traumatic events every day, and they carry those memories forever. But it doesn't mean we stop enforcing the law.

For some reason, when ICE or the Border Patrol arrest an adult accompanying a child and that adult has to be incarcerated, prosecuted, and "separated" from his family, the Left has a fit. Our prison and detention system, along with local and county jails, are filled with adults who are separated from their children. Those who want open borders or no borders at all created a term designed to influence the public: "family separation." Brilliant, right? Who wants families to be separated? Who wants to see videos of crying children? No one. But as with all propaganda, it seeks to cover the truth and sell a lie. The term vilifies the officers for doing their sworn duty to enforce the law. How did we come to the point where the people who knowingly and intentionally violate our laws are the victims and the ones enforcing our laws are the bad guys? Through misinformation and lies. The Left wants a different set of rules for those who violate immigration laws—or no rules at all. Disrespecting our immigration laws for the past several decades created the crisis we see today.

On July 12, 2019, Representative Alexandria Ocasio-Cortez and I had a public chat in a congressional hearing about conditions at border facilities. She thought she had a Perry Mason moment—like she unearthed secret evidence—when she introduced a memo I had signed the previous year recommending a policy of "zero tolerance" at the border. With all the manufactured drama of a Netflix binge of *Law and Order*, she held up a printed page and asked if I was the author of the policy memo. After I pointed out that the document was authored by a group of people, she tried to regroup and asked if I signed it. I calmly answered, "Yes, I signed that memo."

The moment she'd rehearsed with such anticipation had come and gone. There would be no viral video for her today—at least in the way she imagined.

"You recommended family separation," she asserted.

"I recommended zero tolerance."

"Which includes family separation," she continued.

"The same as it is with any US citizen parent that gets arrested with a child."

Interrupting, she went on to argue, "Mr. Homan, with all due respect, legal asylees are not charged with any crime."

"When you're in this country illegally, it's violation 8, United States Code 1325."

"Seeking asylum is legal."

To which I responded, "If you want to seek asylum, you go through a port of entry. Do it the legal way."

After a long pause, she replied with a whimper. "Okay."

You don't have to violate the law and enter illegally to claim asylum. When citizens know the facts about illegal immigration, we can show how shallow and counterproductive some of the Democrats' arguments are. If only more Republicans would join me.

FOURTEEN THOUSAND

In 2014, the number of unaccompanied children was climbing dramatically. That's what happens when people learn there's no real penalty for illegally crossing the border with children—and that there is actually a long list of benefits for doing so. If a child enters alone, and they're from any country other than Mexico or Canada, they cannot be easily removed. It will take years, and the government will release that child to the illegal alien parent or relative that conspired with a criminal organization to smuggle them here. In a way, the federal government was completing the illegal smuggling activity by delivering the child to those who paid to have them smuggled. That is certainly one way to look at it. I have defended ICE in delivering these children to the Office of Refugee Resettlement as not completing the cycle but merely following the law as they are required and as outlined in the Homeland Security Act of 2003 and the William Wilberforce Trafficking Victims Protection Reauthorization Act of 2008.

Jeh Johnson held many meetings with leadership from the operational components, especially the Border Patrol and ICE, when the border numbers surged with family units and unaccompanied children. Many policy advisors were also present. "What would be your law enforcement response or options for slowing this surge down?" they asked.

"First," I answered, "the families who are coming through can't be detained, because we have nowhere to hold them. Border Patrol facilities were never designed for children or family units;

they're basically jails designed to hold men. If we arrest them, then release them into the US in an hour, word will spread and these numbers will go through the roof. We really don't know who they are, if the children are actually theirs, and if they have any illnesses that would endanger the general public if released. The shortage of family detention beds is one of the reasons the number is climbing now—because the word is out that they can't be detained. We need to detain them long enough to see a judge, obtain positive identification, and ensure the children are actually related to the person claiming to be the parent and not a victim of trafficking. Let us build more ICE family detention centers!"

At the time we had only one hundred "family beds" in Pennsylvania at the Burke center. That's all. In the entire country, we could only house one hundred people who claimed to be part of a family unit. There were as many as four hundred family units entering every day. It was catch and release on a grand scale, and we knew the smuggling organizations were using that as a selling point to get more families to hire them. After a long conversation about how these centers are contracted and how they are designed specifically for families, I got the green light.

How do you temporarily house thousands of men, women, and children who endlessly stream over our borders illegally? How could we protect the growing number of children from unrelated adults?

The Border Patrol quickly built temporary facilities to hold the families and unaccompanied children until ICE contractors or the Office of Refugee Resettlement picked up the kids. (During the Obama administration, Congress usually gave the Border Patrol and ICE all the funding we requested. Today, not so much.) We weren't building permanent neighborhoods; these weren't the suburbs. We needed a roof over everyone's head and above all, we needed to keep these people safe from other illegal aliens. These centers have doctors, dentists, child psychologists, schooling for children, recreation, day care, an open-air campus, and free movement. They were far from what you might imagine as a detention center. Within the next eighteen months we built over three thousand family beds. That's right, we *expanded* family detention under the Obama administration. You won't hear that in the media, but it's the truth. Large structures were created by the Border Patrol with chain-link dividers—the same fences that are used to protect children at school playgrounds—that ran all the way up to the tall ceilings.

Was it an elegant solution? No. Was it a perfect solution? Probably not. Were these holding areas "cages"? Absolutely not, and the dedicated men and women of the Border Patrol took exception to that characterization. But that is what the Left wants to call them. They never called them "cages" during the Obama administration, but when the Trump administration used these very same facilities, they screamed about "kids in cages." We needed a way to keep children away from unrelated adults and be in view at all times. Chain-link dividers worked. We rarely knew for certain if "families" were related. Safety and health were always the primary concerns, and these barriers made it simple for agents to monitor and protect children. And crucially, we need to detain people long enough to discover, quarantine, and treat any medical issues.

Call these facilities whatever you want; the Obama administration approved them, funded them, built them, and operated them. And they were operated by the Border Patrol, not ICE. To this day, many open-borders advocates still get that wrong. ICE didn't cage children. But let's face the real issue: fourteen thousand children at one time were in the custody of ORR and being held in licensed care facilities in 2019. These children were separated from their parents, *because of the choices their parents made.* Many of the parents were living and working here illegally, and when the immigration loopholes began to be exploited, these parents decided to hire criminal organizations to smuggle their children here. At the time, everyone on the Left was pretending to care about the 2,500 zero-tolerance separations and how inhumane they were, but at least the kids were taken care of in licensed facilities that were built for children, and not in the hands of a criminal cartel.

Fourteen thousand children were put in the custody of the US government because their illegal alien parents, relatives, or sponsors chose to hire criminal organizations to smuggle them in the trunks of cars, in the backs of tractor trailers, or through the desert on foot. Who would put a kid through that? Can you imagine what the experience does to a young child?

Smugglers took children to the border, pointed north, and told them to look for the green uniforms. Most kids, especially preteens, carried a note in their pocket that read something like, "My name is Alexandria. I want to go to Washington, DC. My parents' address is First St. SE, Washington, DC 20004."

What would you do if you were a Border Patrol agent and confronted with this situation—not once, but hundreds of times per week?

And as soon as word got out that the Border Patrol and ICE were willing and able to detain families, the numbers dropped fast. Detention saves lives.

THE DISCRETION DECEPTION

Open-borders advocates whine that the Border Patrol could use "discretion" when enforcing our laws and simply release families into this country instead of detaining them.

The hard truth is that the parents of these minor children made a choice by crossing the border illegally and placing their children at high risk for injury, abuse, and death at the hands of smuggling cartels. Rather than entering the US through a port of entry, where anyone can claim asylum without violating our laws and where no separations occur, they choose to cross illegally, face prosecution, and have their kids taken away. Children cannot go into US Marshals criminal custody with an adult parent. Eighty-nine percent of all Central Americans who make an asylum claim at the border do not get relief from our courts because they either do not show up in court or they don't qualify under the rules of asylum. Nearly half of those who claim fear at the border never file with the immigration court after being released at the border. Many immigrants deserve our protection, but sadly, most claiming asylum are not being truthful.

When Leftists can't win a logical argument about how to solve the problems on the border, they always resort to emotion. Do they want law enforcement officers to look the other way and exercise "discretion"—or do they really want an open border?

When it comes to the safety of a child, the Border Patrol simply cannot rely on the word of strangers. Law enforcement uses discretion every day, and that's appropriate in certain cases like a speeding ticket. But we can't look the other way when someone chooses to cross a border illegally and chooses to place a child at risk in the process. They must make sure people are who they say they are.

I can't blame anybody for wanting to be part of the greatest country on earth, but you can't be part of the greatest country on earth and not respect our laws. It's simple: According to 8 USC 1325, illegal entry into the United States is a crime. Committing the crime of illegal entry and then immediately committing immigration fraud—that's two crimes—shouldn't be the first thing you do if you respect this country and want to be a part of it.

BUT THEY'RE CLAIMING ASYLUM!

According to the Executive Office for Immigration Review, the courts that make decisions on asylum claims, a vast majority of those claiming asylum are found to not have a credible story, and their requests are denied. Hundreds of thousands of people are fraudulently claiming persecution, and they're bringing children into the deception. We already know that almost half of the families that claim asylum at the border never file a case with the immigration court. Once they're released into the US, they disappear.

Let's talk about where we were before the zero-tolerance policy was put in place. Under the current process, we can't detain illegal aliens long enough for them to see a judge. The Border Patrol is forced to release people into the United States, and few ever appear at their assigned court date. There were more than forty thousand removal orders last year that were handed down in absentia, which means the illegal alien simply did not show up to appear before an immigration judge. If you and I ignored a judge's order, we'd go to jail.

"Bring a child across the border and you'll have a free ticket to the USA and all the benefits we can provide! Don't have a child? You can rent one!" Is that the message we want to send to the world?

People die coming to this country every day, and we keep enticing them with the false promise that we'll look the other way. Conditions in detention are not "inhumane." What's inhumane are parents who choose to put their kids in the hands of smuggling organizations—the same criminal organizations that smuggle guns and drugs. That is inhumane.

Making your claim at a port of entry is not only the legal way to seek asylum, it's the safest way to do it. Doctors without Borders did a study and found that 31 percent of women and girls who make that dangerous journey around legal ports of entry are sexually assaulted. That's one in every three women. Many children die making that journey. And cartels make millions of dollars every day. This illegal smuggling network bankrolls the worst criminal cartels in Mexico. If someone wants to claim asylum with their children, they can walk into the legal port of entry. Our facilities are secure and provide air-conditioning, food, and water—along with professional and caring Customs and Border Patrol personnel who will guide them into the most humane and just legal system in the world.

LEGAL LOOPHOLES

In 2014 and 2015, when families first started coming in mass numbers, ICE built family detention facilities and held these families for around forty days, time enough to see a judge. Nine out of ten did not get judicial relief because they did not qualify for asylum and were ordered removed. They were deemed to be gaming our liberal asylum rules. After their hearings, we quickly put them on a plane and sent them home.

Can you guess what the big-picture result was? My colleagues and I in the Border Patrol saw an immediate and significant decline in illegal family crossings. The Department of Justice took notice and pressed to have this forty-day period legally protected.

That is when Judge Dolly Gee, within the Ninth Circuit Court, decided that we could only detain them for twenty days. In her ruling, she called the Justice Department's effort to extend detention "a cynical attempt" to move immigration policy to the court. The cartels exploited that ruling and started trafficking again, because they knew they would be released before seeing a judge. In my opinion, that single court decision did more harm to this country than any federal ruling that I am aware of in my three-decade career. If these families are in fact escaping fear and persecution from their government, they should be happy to stay in a high-quality facility, safe from the alleged oppression they face in their home countries, until they can plead their case to a judge. When I warned of unprecedented numbers of migrants who'd come into the country if the court was to rule that way, I was called a fearmonger because I had "no evidence." Fast-forward to today. Who was right?

Congress can fix this loophole in one day. Let the government detain illegal alien families in a family residential facility, not a jail—a facility built specifically for families. Again, these centers have doctors, nurses, pediatricians, dentists, child psychologists, day care, three meals a day, new clothes, recreation, visitation, and more. Detainees are not behind razor wire; they are housed in an open campus setting.

We detained them during the Obama administration for around forty days and it worked. The Democrat leadership at the time didn't say a word. But under this president, detention has suddenly become an act of hate? Illegal aliens of all ages who've been released will remain in the US, once again waiting for the next DACA or executive order on amnesty. In 2020, your vote matters.

HEADLINES VERSUS THE FRONT LINES

In the Trump administration, I worked with Attorney General Jeff Sessions on ways to reduce the growing number of illegal crossings. He was serious about the issue and implemented the now-infamous "zero tolerance" policy. I traveled with him to San Diego to make the announcement on May 7, 2018, and our message was simple: Entering the country illegally is a crime, and you will be prosecuted for it.

Was it a big step? Would enforcement get pushback from those who simply didn't understand what was happening? Would the policy be demonized? Yes. But why wouldn't we do everything we can do within the legal framework to save children and adults from dying? Who wants to stand by and shake their heads while thousands of women and children are abused? When do we start cutting the business of human traffickers? The Left seems to have a "tolerance" for all the chaos and pain. I don't.

Zero tolerance went into effect, and all hell broke loose in the media and on Capitol Hill. In hindsight, the messaging wasn't handled as well as it could have been. We should have been clear on why we implemented the policy, what the Border Patrol was doing, and what they were not doing. Photos, videos, and stories of crying children crashed the headlines, and we had to play defense.

In addition to the media frenzy, many Democrats in Congress conveniently withheld the funds requested to quickly build more facilities to address this so-called manufactured crisis.

In 2018, former President Obama called the Trump administration's response a "political stunt," mocking the idea. "The biggest threat to America—the biggest threat!—is some impoverished refugees a thousand miles away." But they weren't thousands of miles away. They were at our doorstep and in our facilities. And we had to release tens of thousands of illegal aliens before their court dates—including court appearances to review their asylum claims.

If you're really escaping fear and persecution from your home country—if you are fleeing death—you shouldn't have any problem staying in the ICE residential facility for a month, or a month and a half, to plead your case to a judge. Right now, there are over 100,000 families defying deportation orders. Only 1 percent have left the US. The only way we can have any integrity in our systems is to detain people, including children, until their case can be tried by a judge.

What you never heard above the screaming was the fact that during the few weeks the zero-tolerance policy was actually enforced, illegal crossings at the Rio Grande Valley went down over 20 percent. How many women were saved from exploitation? How many kids were not abused or killed by coyotes? How many bad guys did we prevent from entering our communities? We'll never know the exact number, but we made a difference.

GENETICS DON'T LIE

In 2017, ICE launched Operation Matador on Long Island to combat gang operations—specifically MS-13. We found that 40 percent of the gang members we arrested came into this country as part of a "family unit." They also posed as innocent, unaccompanied children (even though many were over eighteen years old) and were released into the custody of their "sponsor" who, in some cases, was actually a gang leader.

Recently, the Border Patrol teamed up with ICE and conducted some pilot DNA testing at the border. Tests showed that many of the groups claiming to be families were not actually related. That's right, some of the "family" units traveling together were not genetically linked. Either these groups were a genetic anomaly, or there was human trafficking involved. Imagine if DNA testing was not voluntary but mandated. How many more fake families would be identified?

When I was the director at ICE, we had plenty of cases just like this where cartels and family members would rent children to single adults so they could cross illegally and be released. Incredible, and unthinkable, but very true. HSI even found cases when the same children were "rented" numerous times, so adults could pretend to be their parents and be released into the US. Yes, this actually happens. That's part of the reason we wanted to detain "families," so we could at least try to confirm relationships. Many of the separations were because of reasonable suspicion of a nonrelative claiming to be a parent, which could mean trafficking. Other pilot programs were conducted through extensive interviewing of "family groups," which showed fraudulent claims to be as high as 30 percent, and that many supporting documents were counterfeit.

Obviously, part of the solution to the border crisis involving families is to have mandatory DNA analysis and fingerprinting across the board. The more chilling takeaway from the program was the potential number of children being exploited by cartels. Again, it's the criminals we miss and the victims we don't rescue that keep law enforcement awake at night.

When a judge in San Diego ordered the 2,500 kids in custody to be immediately reunited with their "parents," the government had already started DNA testing on the first 120 children who were ordered to be reunited and found at least 5 percent of the kids weren't related to the adults they entered with. The court didn't want to wait for thorough genetic testing for all 2,500 unless there was additional evidence to proceed with testing, and as a result, hundreds of children may have been released into the custody of human traffickers. A classic, and tragic, example of a catch-22. How can someone claim to care about kids but not empower the Border Patrol to use every means necessary to protect them?

There's a humanitarian reason for sometimes separating children from those claiming to be their parents—especially when the adults choose not to enter legally. There's a commonsense reason for DNA testing. The system is being manipulated. Most of our politicians don't care. It's up to you and me. Now you know the facts. Detention is not inhumane. It's the only way to have order and safety on our border, and inside our country.

ZERO TOLERANCE FOR LAWBREAKERS

Zero tolerance is about more than just enforcing our laws, protecting our sovereignty, and securing our border. It is about saving lives. By implementing zero tolerance, the hope was these family groups would enter through a port of entry, legally, so they wouldn't be in the hands of coyotes. Since the vast majority know they don't really qualify for asylum, maybe more would decide not to make the trip.

For those who claim this administration created "family separation" as a cruel policy against vulnerable populations, I say, you don't know what we know, and you haven't seen what we have seen. You point to a political evil perpetrated by the men and women of Border Patrol and ICE. You march against them, call for their punishment, and bully their wives and children in churches, schools, and restaurants. You call them racists, Nazis, and white supremacists. The actions of the men and women of DHS were never about hate, the policy was always about enforcing the laws enacted by Congress that they took an oath to enforce and doing what they could to save lives and protect those being harmed.

That is what cops do and why they do it, regardless of who is president. Period.

TWELVE

SANCTUARY FOR CRIMINALS

ICE studied New York City for a three-month period, from January to April 2018, and found that police there ignored 440 detainer notices. Within that short period of time, 40 of those individuals released subsequently committed more crimes and were re-arrested.
—CENTER FOR IMMIGRATION STUDIES 2018 REPORT

The man who murdered Kate Steinle in San Francisco had been deported five times and had seven felony convictions.

I never heard of the term *sanctuary city* until around 2013. The term struck me as odd, because if you've ever spent time in one of these cities—not the glitzy tourist areas, the regular neighborhoods—you'll find many of them to be lawless and dangerous. You'll also find that the poorest residents, especially immigrants, live in fear. These communities are not sanctuaries at all—unless you're a criminal alien.

In the early 2000s, while I was the assistant district director for investigations in San Antonio with the INS, we had operational responsibility over a huge part of Texas—from north of Austin to the southern border with Mexico. We received numerous reports and intelligence that many nightclubs and bars in a predominately Hispanic area of Austin were involved in drug dealing and the smuggling of women for prostitution. We planned and carried out an operation on a weekend and hit about eight of those nightclubs, arrested many illegal aliens, and identified some women who were victims of trafficking. Assisting us on that operation was the Texas Alcoholic Beverage Commission, who would suspend licenses of the establishments violating state rules.

I was there to observe the operation and I noticed there were a few Austin police, but they stood in the background and were obviously uncomfortable about assisting the INS. When I asked the INS supervisor about it, he confirmed my hunch. He said the officers wanted to fully engage but would get into trouble if they did. I decided to schedule a meeting with the Austin police chief and see what we could do in order to work better together. A few weeks later I met with the chief, and he was very clear that his officers and his department would not be assisting the INS in the future on operations targeting illegal aliens, even if it involved criminal activity. This was the first time in my twenty-year career that a senior law enforcement leader said that to me. I was flabbergasted when a top-ranking cop looked me in the eye and said that we were on our own.

Some of the less-senior officers in the room were visibly uncomfortable with the conversation. Their body language told me all I needed to know. The street cops were insulted by the pull-back. Little did I know that ten years in the future I'd hear that same line, and worse, from some police chiefs, a few sheriffs, mayors, and other elected officials.

I guess this was a sign of things to come in liberal cities: pandering to certain voter constituencies while violating their oath and abandoning the most vulnerable in immigrant communities and the very citizens they're supposed to protect.

THE LIES AND THE TRUTH

You've heard the arguments. "Sanctuary cities are important because we don't want victims and witnesses of crime to be afraid to approach law enforcement." Leaders of sanctuary cities crow about maintaining the "trust" between the immigrant community and the police. Other politicians say that sanctuary policies help to protect the immigrant community and those most vulnerable. And of course, there's that classic line: "Local police should not do the federal immigration officers' job."

Let's examine the false claim about the protection of victims and witnesses. On the surface, this shallow argument might seem to ring true. After all, an otherwise law-abiding alien may not want to report a crime if they'd be arrested in the process. However, ICE is not looking to arrest any victims or witnesses of crimes. The truth is, ICE wants access to the jail to be notified when a known criminal illegal alien has been arrested and when they will be released. These are people who have been arrested on local or state charges and have been incarcerated because they're deemed either a danger to the public or a flight risk. Again, another law enforcement agency has already arrested them for a crime and locked them in a jail cell. That's the person we want access to.

A sanctuary policy prevents ICE from accessing jails, eliminates notification when an illegal alien is being released from a jail, and prevents local law enforcement from communicating with federal authorities. The result? Bad guys released back onto the street—and most often into immigrant communities. If they were dangerous enough to lock up in the first place, why are they not dangerous enough to turn over to another law enforcement agency, with an administrative warrant, that has probable cause that they've violated federal law?

Let me say this clearly in the hope that the Democrat leadership can understand: ICE is not interested in identifying any victim or witness of a crime.

Unless the police arrest and book a victim or a witness into a jail, ICE would never know of their existence. If victims and witnesses are afraid to report crimes, it's because of the false narrative pushed by pro-immigrant groups, nongovernmental organizations, and politicians who want to vilify the men and women of ICE. They have constantly charged that ICE conducts massive sweeps and arrests all illegal aliens—with no prioritization. Of course, this is a lie. If, by chance, a victim of a crime went to ICE, they could actually be eligible for legal authorization to remain in the United States.

Allowing ICE to access a taxpayer-funded jail to speak to an illegal alien who has been arrested and incarcerated for a crime presents no danger to victims or witnesses. Yet, those who want to knowingly push a false narrative say, "Sanctuary policies protect the immigrant community!" That statement violates common sense, and it is the opposite of what law enforcement sees every day in these cities. When you release a criminal inmate from a local jail, they will usually go back into the very community in which they live to re-offend. This puts the immigrant community at a greater risk of crime. When you look at recidivism rates, you'll find that about 50 percent of those criminals will re-offend within the first year, and as many as 75 percent will re-offend within five years. Why would the local criminal justice system refuse to let the federal officers enforce the law and prevent more people from becoming victims?

A clear example of sanctuary policies in action is how MS-13 gang members operate. Almost all of their activity is within the immigrant community. This means that almost every victim is an immigrant—legal and illegal. Leftist politicians claim to care so much for immigrants, yet they establish policies that handcuff police and put residents in greater danger. If illegal aliens are afraid of anyone in their community, it should be those who put revolving doors on local jails. If you're here illegally but otherwise trying to walk the straight and narrow and live in a sanctuary city, are you going to report crimes to the local police? Of course not. The criminal will be right back on your street, looking for those who informed the cops.

When bad guys are released, it forces ICE agents to go into the community to seek out that criminal. Instead of arresting them in the safety and security of a jail, they must go into the community and places of business to find and arrest the criminal. Not only is this more dangerous for our law enforcement officers, it's much more dangerous for the general public. When ICE is forced into the community to arrest a criminal, chances are they will find others who are illegally in the country. They may be living or working with the criminal alien when we encounter him. These people were not even on ICE's radar until sanctuary policies placed them there. We call these "collateral arrests"—people who are arrested but were not the intended target for arrest. Do you know where most collateral arrests happen? Sanctuary jurisdictions—because we are forced into the neighborhoods rather than operating within a jail. Not only are illegal residents at greater risk of repeat crimes by the offenders, they are at increased risk of ICE arrest.

ICE never asks any local law enforcement agency to be immigration officers. All we want is access to the jail to talk with someone arrested for a crime who may also have outstanding federal arrest warrants. The local jurisdiction can process their case on the subject and simply turn them over to ICE when they're finished. We ask them to honor our detainers, which have been found to be constitutional by the Fifth Circuit Court of Appeals. If they are afraid of lawsuits from the ACLU if they hold persons longer than normal, based on their local charge, they can simply call ICE before they release them. The local jurisdiction already made the decision to lock them up because they are either a public danger or a flight risk. Now, simply let a federal law enforcement officer enforce federal law. Let us do our job. We are the good guys. We want to do our part in helping the local cops keep their communities safe.

As I experienced as both a local cop and Border Patrol agent, law enforcement should always work together to keep our communities safe. That's the oath we all took. There should be no sanctuary for those who intentionally violate our laws. Not only does this policy entice more people to come here illegally, but it also increases the profits of criminal cartels that smuggle people. Let's stop the enticements of sanctuary protection, open borders, free medical care, and other benefits. Instead, let's focus on making our communities safer for everyone. Those who want to illegally come here to commit crimes will almost always choose to live in a sanctuary jurisdiction—where they know they won't be turned over to ICE for deportation, even if they get arrested.

How do politicians tell us with straight faces that sanctuary cities help the immigrant community? We've seen how these policies put the immigrant community at risk for more crime, retaliation against innocent witnesses, and increased risk of ICE arrests. I dare any politician to go to the immigrant community and ask them this one question: "Would you rather have ICE working in your community or the county jail?" Of course, people would rather have agents simply working with local authorities at the jail. ICE agents would also prefer this, because roaming the community puts everyone at greater risk.

A CASE STUDY

Let's talk about just one recent example of the failures of sanctuary policies—one of the most recent and horrific. In Montgomery County, Maryland, nine illegal aliens were arrested for sexual assaults, including rape, within a two-month period in the summer of 2019. Not surprising to me, these were the months immediately following the county's decision to enact the Promoting Community Trust Executive Order, which made Montgomery County a sanctuary county. Seven of the victims were residents of the immigrant community, and many were children. Even after ICE notified the county that they wanted to arrest the criminal aliens, the offenders were knowingly released without turning them over to ICE. The number of rapes in the county have almost quadrupled in the past four years.

How did the "sanctuary city" protect their immigrant community? Countless young lives have been changed, and the trauma will live with them forever. These victims are not statistics or policies—they are human beings. Every crime committed by an illegal alien is a preventable crime if the immigration laws were enforced as intended. Immigrants were the victims of these terrible sex crimes. Again, how did their sanctuary policy protect the immigrant community? It didn't.

In November 2019, after public outcry, Montgomery County officials claimed they altered their policy and allow ICE to have (slightly) more access to the jail. If they follow through, it's a step in the right direction, and it would not have happened without media attention and—most effective—pressure from local residents. Yet just days after this purported change, the county released an illegal alien after booking him on charges of child molestation. We have a crisis on our border and in our communities—and especially in sanctuary cities and counties.

FEDERAL FUNDING

Let's discuss the obvious legal aspect of these so-called sanctuaries. When a city, county, or state chooses to put criminals back onto the street and refuses to partner with ICE, they ignore federal law.

The president and the Department of Justice tried to enforce federal law in these sanctuary areas by withholding grant monies. Of course, the liberal courts stepped in and said it could not be done. The left always shops for the right judge and will file their case in those jurisdictions—many times in the Ninth Circuit. The federal government should be able to withhold funds from communities that choose to ignore our laws and put people at risk. At the time of this writing, the issue is still being appealed. These sanctuary jurisdictions receive federal money to help offset the costs of housing criminal aliens. The program is called the State Criminal Alien Assistance Program. The federal government gives taxpayer dollars to cities to help with their costs, and every year they send in their requests and hold their hand out, saying, "We detained this many illegal aliens; now pay us." But then they refuse to give those criminal aliens to ICE so they can be removed from the country. When they re-offend—and most will—and get locked up again, we will pay again. Talk about senseless. This is just part of the reason that I applaud DOJ for appealing the decisions on sanctuary funding and I believe they will win in the highest courts. Once again, remember that your vote is crucial, because most judges dealing with these matters are appointed by elected officials.

As a special agent, I arrested several US citizens for harboring and concealing illegal aliens in their homes. I've arrested business owners for concealing—and sometimes enslaving—illegal aliens in their place of business. It is a federal felony to knowingly harbor or conceal an illegal alien (8 USC 1324). Again, I have arrested nonpoliticians for this crime. How are cities and counties that harbor and conceal criminal aliens in their jails and refuse ICE access to them any different from those citizens I arrested? Hopefully, the Department of Justice will pursue this further.

When I first mentioned this perspective on sanctuary cities, people shrieked, "Homan wants to arrest politicians!" I never said that. The question is, Why is it a federal crime for a citizen to harbor and conceal illegal aliens, but not a federal crime for a municipality or a politician? Seems like a perfectly rational question. No wonder they want to change the subject. And as far as "knowingly conceal," let me clarify. When someone is arrested and booked, their fingerprints will be taken and run through the FBI's National Crime Information Center to check for criminal history or any warrants. At the same time, those prints are run through DHS databases to search for immigration history. When we get a hit on immigration history and records show, based on these fingerprints, that the person is here illegally, has been deported before, or has an outstanding warrant for deportation, we contact the law enforcement agency that ran the prints and issue a detainer. Therefore, there is no doubt that this person is here illegally and there is no doubt that the jurisdiction holding him knows this, because we informed them. If a municipality ignores this information and refuses to work with ICE, aren't they harboring and concealing those criminals?

DETAINERS

A detainer is a notice we send to the local jail informing them that they have someone in custody who is in the country illegally—and in most cases, other charges pending—and requesting them to hold them after their processing for up to forty-eight hours so ICE can pick them up.

Sounds pretty simple, because it is. And it worked well for over fifty years. Of course, endless lawsuits complicate matters, and I'll spare you most of the boring—and maddening—details. The previous detainer didn't always specify the probable cause on which the request was based. We updated the form to address that concern. Some courts ruled detainers unconstitutional, but the most recent decision on the updated detainer form from the Fifth Circuit court ruled them constitutional in 2018.

Other attorneys and politicians claim that detainers are not legally binding documents because they are "requests," not court orders, and usually not accompanied by warrants. Translation: smokescreen. When Congress wrote the Immigration and Nationality Act (INA), most of the enforcement was administrative in nature, with no actual system to get a criminal arrest warrant from a judge for an administrative arrest. We can certainly charge the person with illegal entry into the United States, which is a crime, and get an arrest warrant, but it's a cumbersome and slow process. In addition, the federal system cannot handle over 12 million criminal arrest warrants and 12 million criminal prosecutions. In practice, by the time a criminal warrant might be obtained, the offender is long gone. That's why more liberal jurisdictions say they need a criminal warrant, because it sounds good to special interests—and because they know we can't get a criminal warrant. As with the issue of not holding those apprehended at the border long enough to have their day in court, the Left loves to play games with the bureaucracy and cheat the law. It's misdirection and misinformation.

Let me be clear, the INA as written and enacted by Congress and signed by a president did not create a mechanism to get a criminal warrant for an administrative arrest. It's not possible, and the law was not written that way. The law was purposely written to give ICE the arrest authority in an administrative process. All the smokescreen and misdirection of those politicians who say "Get a criminal arrest warrant" are either totally ignorant of the law or are choosing to lie to their constituents—or both.

We also added language in the detainer to eliminate confusion and aid compliance. When jurisdictions said they couldn't hold the illegal alien for forty-eight hours, we reminded them to read the new language. The detainer asked to either hold the inmate or notify ICE before release. There's no extra expense, liability, or constitutional question. It's simply a matter of choosing not to work with the federal government. We've asked DOJ to work with the Congress and make the immigration detainer a legally binding document. However, as I've already discussed and will discuss further, Congress currently has no intention of fixing this.

Bottom line, the Left has brainwashed a large segment of our population. ICE is not out to arrest random illegal aliens. The agency is focused on arresting, prosecuting, and eventually deporting those who have entered our country illegally and committed crimes. This past year the data clearly shows that nearly 90 percent of all illegal aliens arrested by ICE in the interior of the US either have a criminal conviction or pending criminal charges at the time of the ICE arrest. We're not talking about hardworking individuals trying to keep a low profile. This is about those who have had DUI, assault, or robbery arrests, for example. In 2019, ICE issued detainers for approximately 2,500 homicides, 56,000 assaults, 14,500 sex crimes, 5,000 robberies, and 2,500 kidnappings. ICE issued 165,487 detainers for criminals in 2019, but the Left wants you to think that ICE doesn't prioritize criminals and is only out to destroy hardworking families. The data doesn't lie, but the Left does.

SANCTUARIES FOR CRIMINALS

ICE tries to raise awareness about the damage sanctuary cities do to society. But you can bet the mainstream media won't report it. For example, in September 2019, acting director Matthew Albence put out one of his excellent reports detailing the consequences. Here are just a few excerpts from the press release concerning the report:

> *"As law enforcement professionals, it is frustrating to see senseless acts of violence and other criminal activity happen in our communities, knowing ICE could have prevented them with just a little cooperation," said Albence. "To the public, who want to live and raise your families in safe neighborhoods, we ask you to hold your lawmakers accountable before you, or someone you love, is unnecessarily victimized by a criminal ICE could have removed from the country."*
>
> *Below are some examples of the risks posed by laws and policies restricting cooperation with ICE:*
>
> - *In September 2019, ICE officers arrested Jose Alejandro Lopez-Gutierrez, 56, in Colorado. Lopez-Gutierrez, a Mexican national, was arrested and booked into the Boulder County (CO) Jail after an arrest for felony sex assault on a child. ICE lodged a detainer on Lopez-Gutierrez in May 2019, but the Boulder County Jail released him from custody three days later without notifying ICE. He had previously been removed on one prior occasion.*
> - *In January 2019, the Mecklenburg County Sheriff's Office (NC) arrested Angel Diaz-Vera, 40, a*

Mexican national, for Driving While Intoxicated (DWI). ICE lodged a detainer, but he was released from local custody. In June 2019, the Mecklenburg County Sheriff's Office again arrested Diaz-Vera for two counts of assault on a female, assault by strangulation, assault with a deadly weapon, and DWI. He again was released from Mecklenburg County despite ICE issuing another detainer and remains at large.

- *In September 2017, Jose Ramirez-Soto, 43, of Mexico, was arrested and booked into King County Jail (Washington) for child molestation charges. In 2018, he was convicted on a sexual assault charge (4th degree). ICE lodged a detainer, but Ramirez-Soto was released. Ramirez-Soto was again arrested and booked in the King County Jail in July 2019 for harassment and threats to kill. ICE again lodged a detainer, but he was released and remains at-large. He has been previously removed from the United States twice.*

- *In July 2019, the Washington County Sheriff's Office (OR) arrested Alejandro Maldonado-Hernandez, 30, of Mexico, for manslaughter, assault and reckless driving. ICE lodged a detainer with the Washington County Jail, but he was released in August 2019 and remains at-large.*

. . . .

Of the nearly 1,300 at-large arrests made this week, ICE officers apprehended 199 people who could have been arrested at a jail if the agency's detainers had been honored. Of all the aliens taken into custody:

- *three (3) had convictions for murder or manslaughter;*
- *100 had convictions for sex crimes—nearly half (47) had convictions for sex crimes involving a minor;*
- *70 had convictions for drug crimes; and,*
- *328 had convictions for driving under the influence.*

"It is past time to put aside all the political rhetoric and listen to the facts—and the fact is, people are being hurt and victimized every day because of jurisdictions that refuse to cooperate with ICE," said Acting Director Albence.

Having been in his position, I can say that ICE could put out a similar report every week.

On June 14, 2019, Charlotte, North Carolina, police arrested Oscar Pacheco-Leonardo on the charges of rape and indecent liberties with a minor. He was accused of having sex with a child under the age of thirteen and was due to report back to court in October. ICE issued a detainer the day after arrest, but it wasn't honored by the Mecklenburg County sheriff's office. The Honduran national, who had been previously deported, was released on June 16. Obviously, had the sheriff honored the detainer, ICE could have taken the criminal into custody. Instead, the community was endangered, as well as the ICE agents who risked their lives locating and arresting him.

In Los Angeles, up to one hundred alien criminals are released every day into the community under California's sanctuary city policy, ICE official Timothy Robbins reported in October 2019.

When you hear stories like this occurring in your community, contact your elected officials immediately. You deserve to know the real story, have the facts, and get the best for every law-abiding resident.

CHAOS IN CHICAGO

During the Obama administration, when I was working with DHS secretary Jeh Johnson, the administration came up with the Priority Enforcement Program (PEP). It basically set the prioritization of ICE to work with jails and get their assistance with felons—but not misdemeanors, unless there were many. I didn't like the narrow prioritization because I believe there are plenty of misdemeanors that are public safety issues, and illegal aliens shouldn't get a pass on them. However, if PEP could get us into sanctuary jails, where we could at least get the felons, it was better than nothing.

During this time, I took a trip to Chicago with the secretary to talk with those in charge of that city, which was one of the biggest sanctuary jurisdictions in the country. We had zero access to the Cook County jail, and we had zero cooperation in the city. The secretary and I met with Toni Preckwinkle, the Cook County Board of Commissioners president, and her staff. Also at the meeting was Jesús García, who was on the board. (I would meet him years later when he was elected to Congress and accused me of being a racist and not caring about dying children because they weren't white.) The secretary did most of the talking and hoped that Cook County would work with us on the new PEP policy, explaining that it simply targeted the worst of the worst criminals. The meeting did not go well, and their resistance was steadfast. The board president claimed that the legal system was racist and only targeted people of color. They were extremely proud to be the first large city in the country to cut all ties to ICE and be a self-proclaimed "sanctuary." The secretary was quick to respond that laws were enforced based on criminal conduct and not race.

The city official's response was the most obvious example of blind ignorance I have ever seen from someone with such authority—and I've seen plenty of ignorance in my career. But I respected the secretary for bringing up the issue face-to-face. Secretary Johnson tried to put the safety of that community over politics, but we were in a room of haters and career politicians. Is it a coincidence that Chicago is now one of the most violent cities in the nation with a record number of shootings? No. Are most victims of those shootings people of color? Yes. Are they doing everything they can to address crime in their city? Of course not. When you refuse to work with other law enforcement agencies, your community suffers. During the Obama administration, ICE arrested and removed thousands of criminals from the streets of Cook County. Why would any elected official put politics over public safety? Again, this is politics at its worst.

SIMPLE SOLUTIONS FOR REAL SANCTUARIES

We're not asking local law enforcement to be immigration cops. We're not asking them to pull cars over and ask people about their immigration status, and we never have. All we're asking them to do is share information on arrested criminals. ICE agents don't want to be cops; we just want access to the jails where those criminals are already locked up. It's that simple.

Section 287(g) of the Immigration and Nationality Act authorizes the Department of Homeland Security (DHS) to deputize local and state law enforcement to enforce our federal immigration law. It also allows DHS and law enforcement agencies to arrange for a four-week training program under ICE supervision, which is paid for by ICE. When I retired we had over sixty jurisdictions in the program and many more on the waiting list. We worked hard to expand that program, and we nearly doubled it.

This program is color blind, in my opinion, because everyone who is booked into a jail through the 287(g) program is screened.

The program is successful because it acts as a force multiplier for ICE and provides them with the resources the Congress has failed to provide. The cooperation benefits the local law enforcement agency because it results in safer communities and fewer criminals released back onto the streets to re-offend.

The National Sheriffs' Association supports the expansion of the 287(g) program, and stated, "It is critical that local law enforce, maintain, and build upon the partnerships with federal law enforcement to ensure that collectively we can promote, protect, and preserve the public safety and homeland security." Sadly, the International Association of Chiefs of Police issued statements opposing participation, claiming it interferes with the "trust, communication, and cooperation" between the immigrant community and law enforcement. By now, you know better. And the cops on the street know better.

The vast majority of law enforcement officers in this country support ICE and honor detainers. The problem lies with elected officials. But it's become our problem, too. I hope this information has emboldened you to speak up and let those elected officials know that sanctuary policies actually hurt every resident—especially immigrants, whose communities are full of criminals who should be in federal custody.

THIRTEEN

THE WAR AGAINST ICE

200

—Conservative estimate of suspected Nazi war criminals arrested and deported by ICE

0

—Number of actual Nazis in US Immigration and Customs Enforcement (ICE)

"Thomas Homan deports people. And he's really good at it." This is a lead line from a 2016 *Washington Post* article. When it was published, I wasn't sure if I was angry or pleased with their description. Today I'm both pleased and upset. If the writer had been with me when I arrested human smugglers, convicted criminals, and gang members, her words might have been a compliment. But I suspect that wasn't the intent. One thing is for sure, I've done my best to follow the law—both the spirit and letter—to protect the people of this country and save lives of both Americans and migrants.

Trust me, no Border Patrol or ICE agent is overjoyed about deporting anyone who is trying to seek a better life for themselves or their loved ones. However, they have a duty to enforce the law and protect our country, even though many aspects of the job can be difficult. We'd much rather the root problem was fixed by Congress. In the meantime, I did my job, served my nation proudly, saved many lives along the way, and advocated (loudly) for solutions.

The men and women of ICE and Border Patrol do their job, every day and night, despite being vilified by the media and elected officials. These agents put their lives on the line for you and me—to arrest criminals and those who intentionally violate our laws and disrespect us as a sovereign nation. These agents leave the safety and security of their homes and their families every day and strap guns to their hips to protect citizens who rarely thank them. They also protect those who hate and vilify them.

When I was ICE director I tried to shake hands and say thank you to every ICE employee I could, especially while doing office visits across the country. I am sure I missed some, but it wasn't because I didn't try. My security detail was well trained and knew they couldn't rush me away from law enforcement officers. While on a northern border tour, we came across a Border Patrol check-point, and my detail said to me, "Director, I assume you want us to stop and walk around and say hi." I smiled and said, "You know it." My security detail sat at my table during meals, because I wanted to talk with them. I never forgot where I came from and what it was like to be on the front line. These were my brothers and sisters—my second family—and family always sits together. Believe me, this was not the norm at the agency before I served. But I was a career cop, and most preceding directors were politicians who didn't serve on the front line.

My special assistant would block off hours every month so I could simply walk around the building one floor at a time and say hello and thank as many folks as I could. I would chat with staff on the elevator and not allow them to be afraid of the boss. I thanked the security guards in our building and tried to ensure they had everything they needed. To this day I'll greet and thank every NYPD officer standing patrol in front of Fox News in New York.

Why am I telling you all this? To prove I was a nice guy who appreciated his colleagues? Okay, I wouldn't mind that. However, my point is that it doesn't take a lot of time or effort to simply say thank you. "Thank you for protecting me and my family so we're safe in our homes. Thank you for serving our country, even on holidays—and for all the birthdays, anniversaries, and first days of school you missed because you were standing post in the middle of nowhere."

These men and women are taking a verbal beating right now from ignorant haters who don't know the real story. They are being called names, and their families are being bullied in schools and churches. They deserve better, and they deserve a simple thank you. If you take anything from this book, please, take this: Say thank you. They would love to hear it.

"THE EXPANSION AND TROUBLING USE OF ICE DETENTION"

On September 26, 2019, I once again ventured before Congress, to testify before a hearing the Democrats titled "The Expansion and Troubling Use of ICE Detention." Yes, really. I never expected a fair or friendly discussion. I was there to defend my brothers and sisters. I was also there to defend the agency and department, along with the private companies that help us detain those who, by law, must be detained. My opening statement read, in part:

> In recent weeks there has been a slew of stories and baseless claims that have compared US immigration customs enforcement facilities to that of notorious Nazi death camps.

That comparison is 100% inaccurate, and it's disgusting. To compare us to the atrocities of the Holocaust . . .

There have been several attacks on our facilities and attacks against our agents and officers. There's also been attacks against our contractors that run these facilities for us.

After more than three decades of enforcing immigration law, I can assure you that if we do not have the ability to detain those that illegally enter our country until they see a judge and plead their case, we will never solve the immigration crisis on the border. Here are a few facts you need to know. I think America would be shocked to know . . .

Nearly nine out of ten people ICE arrests have a criminal history or are pending criminal charges. They are public safety threats.

Our contract facilities have the highest detention standards in the industry . . . I think a lot of taxpayers would be insulted [by] the amount of money we spend on such high standards . . .

I really don't think this hearing is about ICE detention . . . I've been asked, why do I put myself through this, to come up here and be insulted like I have the last two hearings? Because I love the men and women of ICE and Border Patrol, and I know what it's like to wear that uniform and stand on that line, and I will defend the men and women of Border Patrol and ICE until the day I die.

In response to questions later in the hearing, I said:

No one here is talking about how many lives we saved in immigration detention. Many times we're the first doctors these people see. They come to us in bad shape after making a terrible journey. Many times we are providing the first doctor they've ever seen. In our family residential centers we provide the first vaccinations for these children.

As far as the criminals having no impact . . . removing 127,000 criminal aliens from the United States certainly has an impact on less crime in the United States . . . Here is the question that needs to be answered: How many crimes could have been prevented if the illegal alien wasn't here? . . .

You didn't stand in the back of a tractor trailer with nineteen dead aliens who suffocated to death because their smuggler didn't care, including a five-year-old boy. What do you think his last thirty minutes were like? I was there . . . I smelled it, I saw it, and I had a five-year-old boy at the time. And it changed me for the rest of my life. I've seen people who couldn't pay their smuggling fees get stabbed in the face twenty-two times. Thirty-one percent of women are being raped crossing this border, children are dying, cartels are getting rich. Why am I angry? Because you haven't done anything to fix it. Nothing! . . .

You have not seen what I've seen and it's affected me in my life and I've spent my career trying to save lives. When I see what's going on at the southern border right now, and you are ignoring it for political reasons. Why not have a hearing on that? . . .

There is no downside on securing our border. There is no downside on illegal immigration being decreased. There is no downside on less drugs coming into this country . . . ICE seized enough opioids to kill every man woman and child three times. There is no downside to taking money out of cartels hands. None!

I have testified at four congressional hearings since I retired. Democrats are quick to have a hearing when a policy is put in place that may not benefit an illegal alien, but they haven't held one hearing on sanctuary cities or how to secure the border. When I look them in the eyes and ask why, they turn away in silence.

I don't know if my words made a difference with the Democrats that day, but I believe the men and women of ICE and Border Patrol appreciated them. Regardless, the attacks on ICE and their contractors continue. The day I was writing this chapter, another facility associated with ICE was attacked.

A RECENT ATTACK ON ICE

On December 3, 2019, the GEO headquarters office in Boca Raton, Florida, was vandalized by protesters who called for the government to stop doing business with this company and other private detention companies. Numerous protesters blocked the entrance and caused damage to the new building. They threw red paint—to depict blood—all over the building's main entrance and held signs and banners with senseless verbiage. One sign read, "Racist Classist Opportunistic F-ing Prisons."

Protest organizer Nancy Norelli, who was not known to have participated in any illegal acts, released a statement saying activists "from a myriad of organizational backgrounds came together to physically impede 'business as usual' at GEO's corporate office. The for-profit company's government contracting services have led to 'the suffering of children' and should be terminated. We will not allow their workers to sit undisturbed in air-conditioned offices while people are deprived of their humanity, dying in crowded cages."

I have a message for Norelli and her comrades: Read a book. Educate yourself. Read the Homeland Security Act of 2003, and you'll find that the law dictates that ICE and Border Patrol must turn unaccompanied children who enter the US illegally to the Department of Health and Human Services (HHS) within seventy-two hours. HHS, by statute, must detain those children. Seems like these protesters don't have a job, so they decided to stumble out of their parents' basements and prevent others from working.

THE WAR ON ICE

In 2019, senator and presidential candidate Kamala Harris said the ICE raids were the administration's "campaign of terror." The mainstream media loves to parrot the slander of the Left. But they won't talk with me. Did you know I've never been asked to appear on MSNBC, *Meet the Press*, *This Week*, *Face the Nation*, or most other popular news outlets? When I was on CNN in 2018, Wolf Blitzer wouldn't respond to the series of verifiable facts I presented to him. I haven't been on that network since.

You'd think that as ICE director and afterward, I'd be called on to bring perspective. But as radio host Mark Levin pointed out, I've basically been censored from newsrooms. Meanwhile, the uninformed have an open mic every day. But I was the first ICE director to come up through the ranks. I know this game, and no one's going to beat me at it.

Alexandria Ocasio-Cortez was one of the first to call for the abolishment of ICE. She may have been a good bartender in her day, but she's a terrible representative in Congress. In my opinion, every time she talks about immigration, she's wrong. At least she's consistent. Yet her voice is all you hear on mainstream media. Federal law enforcement has done more to protect the residents of New York than she ever will. During my first year as ICE director, we took over five thousand criminals—who previously walked out of their sanctuary city jails—off the streets of New York. Her community is safer because of ICE. You are welcome, Alexandria Ocasio-Cortez.

In February 2018, while I was ICE director, Representative Nancy Pelosi released a statement condemning ICE enforcement actions in her district: "The Trump Administration's raids were a shocking abuse of law enforcement power. Yet again, the White House has reached into our communities to indiscriminately detain scores of hard-working, law-abiding immigrants."

Notice that her comments are directed toward the "Trump Administration." I can tell you, because I was in the Obama administration for many years, she never made statements like this when similar enforcement actions were taken during the previous administration.

Pelosi continued: "Fully half of those swept up in the ICE raids have no criminal record. This raid was intended solely to terrorize innocent immigrant families and instill fear in the hearts of our communities—not to keep Americans safe. Parents will now be torn from their children, and spouses ripped away from their loved ones."

She is actually accusing the men and women of ICE of carrying out these arrests for the sole purpose of terrorizing families. ICE agents are human beings—some of the finest I've ever known.

And more Pelosi garbage: "The Administration continues to brazenly target the cities that refuse to bow to its blatantly bigoted anti-immigrant and mass deportation agenda. The people of the San Francisco Bay Area will continue to oppose these cowardly attacks, and we will remain open to the patriotic immigrants who are the constant reinvigoration of America."

Again, she calls the actions "cowardly" and thereby calls the agents cowards. Yet, in her mind, the criminal aliens are "patriotic." As far as I know, Nancy Pelosi has never been on our southern border. She meets with immigration advocates all the time, defends MS-13 gang members, but when I was Director of ICE, she refused to meet with angel moms and dads in her district. She and her colleagues Chuck Schumer and Debbie Wasserman Schultz would not meet with me.

To the Speaker of the House and others who parrot this hatred: ICE does not arrest innocent people. They arrest people who are in the country in violation of federal law—laws that Pelosi and her colleagues are free to change. Regarding her delusion about a "mass deportation agenda," ICE removed many more people under the Obama administration than we have during the Trump administration, and she never said a word.

If the Democrat Party and the so-called journalists have their way, there'll be no border. There'll be no new wall, and ICE will be abolished or transitioned into something useless. The Border Patrol will be turned into a massive day care center where they hand out voter registration cards for the Democrat Party. And this society, this country, will be destroyed.

ICE was created in 2003 after 9/11. It has about twenty thousand employees. There are three major branches within ICE. Homeland Security Investigations does criminal investigations enforcing over four hundred criminal statutes. Enforcement and Removal Operations carries out immigration laws within the United States. The Office of Principal Legal Adviser, our attorneys, prosecute immigration cases in immigration court. Those calling for ICE to be abolished either have no idea what the agency really does, or they're simply playing political games—or both.

They want to abolish an agency that rescued hundreds of women from sex trafficking last year and saved thousands of children from child predators and traffickers. They want to abolish an agency that seized enough opioids to kill every man, woman, and child in this country three times over. They want to abolish an agency that's the number one participant with the FBI and

Joint Terrorism Task Force in terrorism investigations. They want to abolish the agency that does gun-trafficking investigations, narcotics investigations, technology and weapons smuggling investigations. They want to abolish the agency that has a civil rights division, where we have removed hundreds of *actual* Nazis from the United States over the years and sent them back to face trial. We have removed hundreds of human rights violators to their home countries so they can stand trial for their crimes against humanity.

They want to abolish the agency that arrested 137,000 criminal aliens last year. These are illegal aliens who committed a criminal violation while here. Under the Obama administration, approximately 59 percent of those removed had a criminal history. Under the Trump administration, the percentage of arrests of those with a criminal record is near 90 percent. This is proof that the Trump administration targets criminals.

Congress would rather abolish an entire federal law enforcement agency than fix the laws. Whose job should be eliminated— ICE agents or these elected representatives?

I have a simple request for my next congressional testimony. Let's have these representatives also placed under oath, and allow me to ask them a few questions. That would set the record straight for sure. By the way, we can all contact them and ask questions— and I hope you will! They work for us. Instead of making political speeches and grandstanding for a viral YouTube moment, they should answer to us and do the job they are paid to do.

ICE VERSUS POLICE POLITICIANS

In October 2019, a Fairfax County, Virginia, police officer was suspended for turning an illegal alien over to ICE. The illegal alien caused the accident, had no driver's license, carried no insurance, and had an outstanding warrant. The Fairfax County police chief made the decision to suspend the officer, and said "This is an unfortunate issue where the officer was confused. We have trained on this issue a lot. This is the first time we've had a lapse in judgment, and the officer is being punished." To add insult to injury, the chief added that the officer, "deprived a person of their freedom, which is unacceptable."

The cop was being a cop. Maybe the chief ought to remember what it's like to be a cop. In my view, the chief stopped being a cop when he made that decision. He became a politician.

How many criminal aliens has ICE taken off the streets of Fairfax? Law enforcement is supposed to work with law enforcement. It's about keeping the community safe. If that warrant had been from the FBI or DEA, or from another county or city, this wouldn't have happened.

Our world is upside down when those who illegally enter the country in violation of the law are the victims and the ones who enforce law are the bad guys. Thankfully we have a president who is working to turn things right side up. And thankfully, Roessler reversed the suspension, but only after public outcry.

I'll say it again, and I hope he reads it: To me, the chief stopped being a cop that day. He became a politician. A police chief or sheriff must remember that their number one responsibility is to protect their communities. When any law enforcement official knowingly releases a criminal back to the streets to re-offend rather than taking a legal option of turning him over to ICE, they have failed their community. If I was ICE director today, I'd hire that Fairfax officer and be proud to have him on our team.

FICTION VERSUS FACT

Let's put something in perspective: The agency is doing the same job they've been doing for decades, before they were called ICE and were the Immigration and Nationalization Service. They've always arrested those who are in the country illegally and in violation of the law. About 89 percent of everyone they arrest has a criminal history or a criminal conviction.

I didn't see the hateful narrative in 2012, during the Obama administration, when ICE removed 409,000 illegal aliens, an all-time record. The three and a half years I was the executive associate director for enforcement and removal operations at ICE—under the Obama administration—I oversaw the deportation of 1 million illegal aliens. President Obama gave me a Presidential Rank Award because of my work. Where was all the hate and rhetoric then? If Democrats were honest, they'd admit two truths: They're grateful someone does the thankless job of deporting criminal aliens (drug smugglers, human traffickers, and gang members), and the reason they're so publicly opposed to ICE is simply hatred of our president. Think about that for a moment. These politicians hate our president so much that they'd rather see him fail, keep the border in chaos, and have criminal aliens released into the streets than do their job. Their desire to see him fail has taken over their souls.

No one wants to talk about the hate that the ICE agents and their families deal within their communities. It's disgusting on every level, and it's based on a false narrative being pushed by the Left and certain members of Congress. They despise law enforcement—especially agencies that secure our borders and enforce our immigration laws. It sickens me, not only as a career law enforcement officer, but as a US citizen. Those who choose to put themselves in harm's way and defend this nation deserve our respect, not our hate.

Let's set the record straight with facts.

ICE has never arrested a child at school. The agency has never pulled a child out of school and arrested them. In addition, ICE has never arrested a child, or a parent, on school grounds. Has ICE arrested a parent *after* they've dropped their child off at school? That's happened a few times, but only after the agents have done their own research to make sure there was a parent available to pick up that child after school, and in cases of priority arrest involving a criminal history.

No illegal alien has ever been arrested in a church by ICE.

ICE has not arrested an illegal alien in the hospital. However, the Left and much of the media will claim that illegal aliens are afraid to go to school, church, or medical centers. If there is fear, it's because of the lies that many Democrats have spread for their own political gain.

ICE doesn't make indiscriminate arrests in the communities. Nine out of ten people arrested have a criminal history or have criminal charges pending. ICE does not conduct indiscriminate raids or sweeps. When ICE arrests someone in a community, it's a targeted enforcement operation. They know who they are going to arrest, and they have a plan for where they're going to arrest them. These agents regularly receive Fourth Amendment training and are fully aware of the legal boundaries. Agents do not comb the streets looking for people to randomly arrest. For every person originally targeted for arrest, a fugitive operation plan is created. This may include information about children, so they try not to arrest parents when their children are present, except in extreme circumstances when serious criminal activity is an issue for the family or community. They do their homework and do a very good job of it.

During an arrest operation, sometimes agents find other illegal aliens. These are called collateral arrests. Where do most collateral arrests happen? They happen in sanctuary cities. Why is that? Sanctuary cities do not allow us to arrest the bad guy in a jail, which means ICE has to go to the neighborhood to arrest the bad guy—where ICE will more than likely find others. Again, sanctuary policies put the immigrant community at greater risk of arrest.

ICE arrested or removed 137,000 criminals—public safety threats—last year. These aren't people who are "just" here illegally; they are convicted of a crime in addition to an immigration-related crime.

ICE fugitives account for only one in ten arrests. These are people who enter the country illegally in violation of the law, are given due process at great taxpayer expense, and ordered to leave the country by a judge, but don't leave. This country spends billions of dollars each year on border security, detention, immigration court, appellate court, and circuit court. After the hearing, the law is clear that ICE's responsibility is to execute those orders. If our laws can be ignored at will, there will be no integrity in our entire justice system. You might as well fire all the Border Patrol agents and open the border, because there is no accountability, no consequence, and no deterrence to breaking the law. What would happen to a US citizen if they simply ignored a judge's order? You know the answer. But some Democrat politicians hold press conferences on how illegal aliens can evade arrest by ICE, and mayors refuse to assist ICE. They think we can pick and choose what laws we obey. I'll keep that in mind if I ever get a parking ticket in Chicago.

Last year, ICE seized enough opioids and fentanyl to kill every man, woman, and child three times over. ICE rescued over seven hundred women from sex trafficking. ICE has rescued thousands of children from sexual predators. ICE places several thousand sexual predators in jail every year and prevents countless assaults.

ICE stops technology from being smuggled out of the United States, including sensitive military technology that could be used against us and our soldiers on the battlefield. Counter-proliferation investigations are one of the most important aspects of ICE's work.

ICE is the second-largest supporting agency of the FBI and performs a number of joint terrorism investigations. ICE has arrested terrorists and prevented terrorists from coming to this country.

ICE runs the visa security program and has prevented tens of thousands of people from obtaining a visa to come to this country and do us harm. Because of the excellence of ICE investigators, it is much harder for a terrorist to game the system.

ICE arrests and removes criminals who are wanted in their home countries for human rights abuses. These crimes include some of the most heinous acts, and ICE will not allow this country to provide them sanctuary. Over the past two decades ICE arrested and removed hundreds of Nazi war criminals and other human rights violators and sent them back to face trial for the terrible acts they committed during and after World War II.

ICE is part of many gang task forces. The brave agents have removed thousands of gang members, including thousands of MS-13 members, who have brutally attacked people in this country. The victims are most often other illegal aliens.

This is who ICE is. Remember these facts the next time someone screams about abolishing the agency.

CHANGING THE NARRATIVE

It's no wonder that public sentiment has, to a larger extent than I ever imagined, turned against ICE. We're bombarded with lies and twisted arguments every day. You and I must stand up to the lies and tell the truth. I hope the facts in this chapter, and this book, embolden you to vote for those who respect our laws and encourage friends and family to do the same.

You may not want to sign up, put on a Kevlar vest, strap a gun to your hip, and wear an ICE or Border Patrol badge, but you can still have their backs.

Imagine being an ICE agent and having to arrest an at-large criminal—someone who's in the country illegally and just committed murder, assault, or robbery. You're going to try to arrest someone who doesn't want to be arrested. How many Americans would do that job, knowing it could lead to a life-and-death struggle? An ICE or Border Patrol agent has to face this scenario all the time. Most people have never been in a fight in their life, whether it's in a schoolyard or at a bar. ICE Agents expect a fight and plan for it. How many people would do that job?

I've served under six presidential administrations with the finest people in this country. The job they've been asked to do hasn't really changed. What's different is how the Democrat leadership views both the law and law enforcement officers. The attacks need to stop. It's only a matter of time before one of their verbal attacks leads to actions that will result in the death of an agent. The blood of that agent will be on the hands of many of those on the Left who spread lies and stir anger.

Hate groups do exist on all sides of the political spectrum. But in just a decade, a new hate group has formed—those who hate ICE, the Border Patrol, and all involved in enforcing our immigration laws.

The Left has created a group of legislators and congress-people who hate law enforcement with blind rage—for political gain. I've experienced it firsthand, and so has my family. As I've mentioned, a group of eighty protesters showed up in front of my home and shouted the worst insults and threats you can imagine. They thought they would make me go away or shut up. Good luck with that. And for those who disrespect law enforcement officers, who do you think they'll call when they're in danger? The very law enforcement officers they hate. Because cops run toward danger when everyone else runs away.

Antifa shut down our ICE building in Portland for weeks. They took down the American flag and put up the Antifa flag. In a Colorado detention facility, they took down the American flag and raised the Mexican flag. These hateful protesters want open borders but are completely ignorant about the realities on the ground— and the consequences of their policies. When they can't get a job and their wages are stagnant, will they protest? When there's a long line at the local medical trauma center, will these protesters connect the dots? When their children share a classroom with fifty other students instead of twenty, will they understand how illegal immigration affects ordinary families? When a violent criminal is released into their sanctuary city—into their neighborhood—will they speak up?

Enforcing our laws isn't just about securing the border; it's about saving lives and improving our quality of life. To paraphrase the *Washington Post*'s line, ICE deports dangerous criminals, and they're really good at it.

If Leftists politicians truly understood what ICE does and doesn't do, I'd like to imagine they would shake agents' hands and thank them for putting their lives on the line. Maybe someday. But in the meantime, you and I can.

FOURTEEN

THE TRUMP EFFECT

In the first full month of my administration following the issuance of my executive orders, illegal immigration on our southern border fell by an unprecedented 40 percent.
—PRESIDENT DONALD TRUMP

Apprehensions on the border went from 66,708 in October of 2016, to 16,588 in March of 2017.
—US CUSTOMS AND BORDER PROTECTION

From the time I was a little kid, I always looked up to cops. Then I became one, and I respected law enforcement even more. During my time as a federal agent, I always stood up for cops. On November 21, 2019, I was honored as Man of the Year by *Blue* magazine, Moment of Silence, and Brothers before Others in a New Jersey "Night to Unite" ceremony. Weeks before, when these organizations came together and announced that I'd receive the award, I had a meeting in the White House. As I entered the Oval Office, the president congratulated me. I had a few copies of *Blue* magazine with me and showed him the cover, which featured a photo of me addressing reporters in the White House press corps briefing room. My facial expression was, as in many photographs, one of intense frustration.

I asked the president to sign two copies, so I could give one back to the cops who publish the magazine to display in their offices. He grabbed a pen and wrote, "Tom, You are Great" along with his signature, then signed a copy for the magazine. *Blue* is an independent publication that's owned and operated by police officers. They write stories about the inherent dangers of the job, issues with law enforcement in today's culture, along with the struggles and successes of being a cop. They placed my not-smiling mug on the cover and featured an interview with me. This was a testament to the fact that people are listening, and it gives me the strength to continue fighting, continue talking, and continue yelling until people understand what is happening to our country.

Moment of Silence is a nonprofit organization of and for police officers. I try to stay away from distinctions of "active" or "retired" because I strongly believe *once a cop, always a cop*. You may hang up your gun and badge after a long career but your heart will always be blue. Moment of Silence facilitates educational programs designed to improve and encourage the overall safety of first responders and military—and supports the children of those who've fallen in the line of duty. They also lobby the government to pass legislation that supports first responders. One of their biggest priorities right now is shining a light on the terrible tragedy of suicide among police, which is happening on an epidemic scale these days.

Brothers before Others is also a nonprofit organization comprised of policemen and policewomen. This charitable group provides a floral arrangement to every fallen officer's department and family, ensuring that no line-of-duty death goes unnoticed. They also provide a social media platform for cops to communicate with one another.

The night before this event I had dinner with many of the organizers of the event, including the Woman of the Year award recipient, Michelle Malkin. She is another outstanding spokesperson for law enforcement, especially ICE and the Border Patrol. I am proud to call her a friend.

I've received many awards during my long career, most notably the Presidential Rank Award for distinguished service in 2015, the highest award given by a president to a civilian. I also received the Distinguished Service Medal in 2018. However, the two honors that meant the most to me were from those who serve on the front line each and every day. I was given the Law Enforcement Person of the Year Award in 2018 by the twenty-thousand-member-strong Federal Law Enforcement Officers Association, an organization made up of numerous federal agents and law enforcement professionals.

And the icing on the cake was this Man of the Year Award given by front-line cops at Night to Unite—a tremendous event, with nearly one thousand cops in the same room. The camaraderie was tremendous, but it's always that way with police and firefighters. The men and women of the profession I admired as a child—and had the privilege to join—took time from their busy lives to say thank you. It doesn't get any better than that. And yes, I was moved to tears a few times during that evening—especially when the bagpipes started wailing "Amazing Grace" for all who've fallen.

All my life I wanted to make a difference, and pursue greater impact—from my time as a local cop in small-town New York, to the Border Patrol, to retirement, to un-retirement, to ICE Director. I've advised in the Oval Office and on Air Force One, and I've been thanked by the president for my service on several occasions. My life and career came full circle that day.

One of the highlights was being introduced by Bernie Kerik, the finest police commissioner New York City ever had. He was the top cop who handled the 9/11 attack with strong leadership and professionalism. I told the audience it was an honor to be handed the award by the man I used to watch on TV during the weeks of the 9/11 emergency response. I shared how I used to see him at the podium during those many press briefings, and even though I hadn't met him, I could tell by the look on his face and the way he spoke that he had this. And he did. His leadership helped this country heal.

Much of my acceptance speech was about President Trump and his love and respect for the men and women who serve on the front lines. Until you serve, you don't realize what a thankless job it can be and how much a thankful leader means.

STORIES OF LEADERSHIP

That evening, I heard numerous stories about Donald Trump, from his life before 2016. I learned how he supported law enforcement long before he became president. Bernie Kerik shared with me that Trump used to go down to Ground Zero in the dark of the night in the aftermath of the September 11 attacks on New York City. He was on the scene within hours and sent workers from his numerous construction projects to Ground Zero to assist in the rescue efforts. He was an icon in New York City at the time, and every cop knew him. There was no press; he wasn't there for a photo op. He went among the debris and hazardous conditions to personally thank the men and women doing the incredible task of respectfully recovering remains so family members could honor the deceased. That's right, a billionaire businessman went to that scene where so many perished, and so many got sick, simply to pay his respects—not once, but numerous times.

An officer named Rob told me a story about working for the New York City Transit Police, before they merged with the NYPD, in the midtown Manhattan area. He and other officers had numerous interactions with then businessman Trump, who always noticed Rob and the other officers, stopped what he was doing, and asked how they were doing. He'd tap them on the chest or back to make sure they were wearing their bullet-resistant vests and remind them to "be safe." Trump would also extend invitations for them to use Trump Tower's employee dining facilities for their lunch or dinner break. According to Rob, it was obvious that some of his executive staff in their $3,000 suits looked unfavorably at civil servants eating in their dining space, dressed in their uniforms or shoddy plain clothes.

One day, Trump took Rob and another officer aside and asked them, "Have you eaten at the Tower facility lately?" They thanked him and told him they had. He then asked them to give him an honest critique of the food and facility, saying, "Most of the people I ask just tell me 'yes' and 'fine'—but I know the guys in the NYPD won't BS me."

Rob told him everything was great, but in a joking manner mentioned that "a soft-serve ice cream bar would be nice." A few weeks later, a spectacular ice cream bar appeared. Knowing that some of his staff didn't always appreciate the cops in their dining hall, Trump placed a sign above the installation that read, "You can thank the men & women in Blue for this ice cream bar. Because of their honesty and suggestions we have added this selection for all to enjoy."

But this was about much more than ice cream. According to Rob, by doing this Trump changed the mindset of his corporate staff. Cops went from being tolerated to celebrated. Within a few days, two executives dressed in those pricey suits approached him and his crew, thanked them for their service, thanked them for the ice cream, and added, "If you don't mind, could you mention to Mr. Trump that a Santa Fe salad bar would be great?"

I heard countless stories about Donald Trump that night—the man, not the celebrity or the president. From showing up at police fundraisers in the late eighties and nineties to say thank you and hanging out with those in attendance, while quietly leaving hefty donations, to everyday interactions with street cops.

During my speech, as soon as I mentioned President Trump I was interrupted by loud applause. The thousand-strong crowd of cops love our president. At the end of my speech I grabbed my phone, started recording video, and asked them to say hi to the president who "has their six." Shouts turned into chants of "USA" for several minutes. The feelings are mutual, Mr. President. The respect and love you have for our police are returned to you a thousand times over, sir.

The Trump effect is pro–law enforcement.

THE TRUMP EFFECT ON THE BORDER

It's remarkable what good leadership brings, to a community and a country. Border crossings plummeted after Trump was elected in 2016. Apprehensions on the border went from 66,708 in October 2016—the month prior to the election—to 16,588 in March 2017. That's about a 75 percent drop in five months. Donald Trump said what he meant and meant what he said—and people on both sides of the southern border took notice.

Those considering illegally immigrating to the United States might have assumed the Republican-led Congress would make good on campaign promises, support the electorate, and address the crisis. Sadly, very little changed in Washington, especially among the career politicians.

Soon, cartels, gangs, and illegal aliens realized Congress was still paralyzed and self-absorbed. And the number of crossings went back up.

In 2018, when Democrats won the majority in the House of Representatives, the numbers climbed even higher, and the situation became a full-blown crisis. Tens of thousands of family units and unaccompanied children flooded the border, assisted by gangs and cartels. The freshmen Democrats gained power and yelled "abolish ICE" and "detention is cruel." And we know what effect their "leadership"—or more accurately, their lack of any leadership—had on the border crisis. But there is some good news to report as well.

In the fall of 2019, apprehensions at the Rio Grande Valley sector were down significantly compared to the previous summer. Initiatives like "Remain in Mexico" (MPP) and some increased cooperation from the Mexican government have helped. These numbers have gone up and down over the past three years, but it shows how clear, committed leadership on the issue of illegal immigration can make a huge difference on the border—great leadership by President Trump. He deserves the credit.

The president declared a national emergency to secure additional funding to address the crisis, even though some in his own party disagreed with him. He made deals with El Salvador, Guatemala, and Honduras. He unveiled a comprehensive immigration reform plan in May 2019, which we'll detail in the next chapter, and Congress has yet to discuss it.

I've worked under six different presidential administrations: Reagan, Bush, Clinton, Bush, Obama, and Trump. They all handled immigration differently, but this fact doesn't change: The person in the Oval Office greatly impacts the people on the front lines of law enforcement. The president sets the tone—either by what they say and do, or by what they don't say and don't do.

President Reagan was fairly strong on immigration. President Clinton was decent on immigration because he actually talked about how we need to secure our borders. Listen to Clinton's state of the union speech in 2006, and you'll hear that he advocated for secure borders and said illegal employment needs to stop. They all talk the talk. President Trump walks the walk.

2016 AND TODAY

I announced my first retirement in October 2016 while I was the executive associate director at ICE, the number three in command, because I was convinced Hillary Clinton was going to win the election. I wasn't going to put up with four more years of political games on the border. I gave the Obama administration ninety days' notice, because the position is not easy to fill.

Candidate Trump gave a speech in Phoenix in August 2016 on the topic of immigration and presented ten ways to end the illegal immigration crisis. Even though I thought he had a snowball's chance in the heat of the election, I took notice. Here are some excerpts from his address.

> *Tonight is not going to be a normal rally speech. Instead, I am going to deliver a detailed policy address on one of the greatest challenges facing our country today: immigration . . .*
>
> *But to fix our immigration system, we must change our leadership in Washington. There is no other way. The truth is, our immigration system is worse than anyone realizes. But the facts aren't known because the media won't report on them, the politicians won't talk about them, and the special interests spend a lot of money trying to cover them up.*
>
> *Today you will get the truth.*
>
> *The fundamental problem with the immigration system in our country is that it serves the needs of wealthy donors, political activists and powerful politicians. Let me tell you*

who it doesn't serve: it doesn't serve you, the American people.

When politicians talk about immigration reform, they usually mean the following: amnesty, open borders, and lower wages.

Immigration reform should mean something else entirely: it should mean improvements to our laws and policies to make life better for American citizens. But if we are going to make our immigration system work, then we have to be prepared to talk honestly and without fear about these important and sensitive issues.

For instance, we have to listen to the concerns that working people have over the record pace of immigration and its impact on their jobs, wages, housing, schools, tax bills, and living conditions. These are valid concerns, expressed by decent and patriotic citizens from all backgrounds.

We also have to be honest about the fact that not everyone who seeks to join our country will be able to successfully assimilate. It is our right as a sovereign nation to choose immigrants that we think are the likeliest to thrive and flourish here.

Then there is the issue of security. Countless innocent American lives have been stolen because our politicians have failed in their duty to secure our borders and enforce our laws . . .

Anyone who tells you that the core issue is the needs of those living here illegally has simply spent too much time in Washington.

Only out of touch media elites think the biggest problem facing American society today is that there are 11 million illegal immigrants who don't have legal status.

*To all the politicians, donors and special interests, hear
these words from me today: there is only one core issue in
the immigration debate and it is this: the well-being of the
American people. Nothing even comes a close second . . .*

*We will treat everyone living or residing in our country
with dignity. We will be fair, just and compassionate to all.
But our greatest compassion must be for American citizens.*

He went on to talk about policies that he would put in place to
defend our border and enforce immigration laws. I sat there truly
amazed, because I've never heard a president talk this clearly about
the crisis, and because I couldn't have presented a better case to
the voters.

Then Trump won. I guess other people were listening, too.

President Trump was the first president I've seen who understood the immigration issue inside and out. Why? Because he has
common sense, he cares about citizens, and he spoke to the experts.
During my time in the Obama administration, I was number three
at ICE, and the president never asked for my input. Not only that,
my superior at the agency never had a meeting with the president
on the topic of immigration.

In the Trump administration, we spoke at least every two
weeks. He didn't forget about his campaign promises; he expected
results from me and everyone on his team. He wasn't content to
throw a policy idea out, say, "Okay, go run with it," and forget
about it. He held us accountable like no one I'd ever worked with
in Washington. He showed true leadership like I have never seen
before in Washington, DC.

In our trips to the southern border, he'd sometimes walk right
by the chief to shake the hand of a front-line officer. He wanted

to hear from the men and women doing the job. "How's it going? What can we do better?" No other president gave these agents the time of day. This leader listens. You can write all the policy papers you want, but unless the solutions are practical where the rubber meets the road, they make no difference.

If Americans could have been in the room with us on so many different occasions and heard his ideas, his love for our country—and yes, his love for immigrants—their support would go through the roof. Law enforcement morale is up from its lowest point in thirty years. Border Patrol morale is high. ICE morale is high because we are getting to do the job we signed up for. You want to fight this president? Have at it. I think he likes fighting. I think he loves to fight for the right cause—especially protecting our country—and he loves to win.

I have also been with President Trump on numerous occasions when he met with angel moms and dads. He listens to them and assures them that he will keep fighting for them. This is yet another side of this president that the media will never show. As the ICE director, I met with these parents many times and attended their events to bring attention to illegal alien crime and the needless loss of life. No parent should ever have to bury a child, but for your child to be killed by someone who is in the country illegally multiplies the heartache. They know that if we had true border security and enforced immigration laws, their children might still be alive.

One of the first actions Donald Trump took when he became president was to create the Victims of Immigration Crime Engagement office within ICE, which helps victims and their families receive help and information about their cases. Can you believe this support never existed before? That's just another example of why the 2020 election is so crucial.

THE 2020 EFFECT

We've got to keep Donald Trump in office in 2020. If we don't win, the border is in big trouble, and so is our country.

I've seen more massive changes on the border in the last three years than I've ever seen in my entire career. This president is trying to maintain the rule of law. Every Democrat nominee wants to ignore those laws, erase the border, and buy votes from immigrants with an endless list of free enticements. They want the power of the White House for the foreseeable future. So they want future votes.

The more people who are counted in the census means more seats in the House of Representatives. That's why the Democrats are pushing back on the citizenship question on the current census. They've argued that the count would be artificially low because those here illegally will not participate. But these politicians want every person in this country, legally and illegally, counted as citizens because it will expand their power. Most illegal aliens reside in liberal districts, which would mean more Democrat congressional seats and more sway in the electoral college.

These career politicians care more about their reelection and political power than they do about this nation's sovereignty and your safety. They hate this president more than they love this country.

Even if you don't particularly like the president's outspoken personality, do you really believe the Democrats' policies and passive-aggression toward citizens will help this country? The choice is day and night. If you believe in the sovereignty of the United States, if you believe we have the right to defend our border, if you believe a country is not a country unless it has borders, then you have no other choice.

Please believe me, as someone who loves this country and whose career has taken him from the dirt roads of the border to Air

Force One. If a Democrat wins the 2020 election, it's not like we'll go back to the way things were during the Obama administration. Don't kid yourself, and don't let your friends kid themselves. If one of the current Democrats running for president actually becomes president in 2020, the situation on the border will go from bad to unimaginable. And the chaos will not be limited to the border. Every state and every community in our country will be negatively impacted—at a speed that goes beyond your worst fears.

A wide-open border degrades everything in this country: health care, schools, public safety, social services, the economy, wages, and national security. And, if we don't hold this ground, in ten to twenty years our elections will shift forever into the blue. Democrats want power. They'll get it, and they'll hold it—for decades.

Don't believe me? Read the headlines. People who violate our immigration laws are now "victims." And those who enforce the laws that Congress passed are the "bad guys." What effect would a Democrat win have on the morale of law enforcement—on the border and on your street? You know the answer.

This election is about keeping our country, and it's about law enforcement. Law enforcement is under attack. I don't think you can vote for the Democrat candidate and be pro–law enforcement. And you can't sit this election out. And I'm not just talking about the presidential election; we need pro-America officials on our school boards, city councils, and in county and state governments. This is a ground-level effort.

We have a great president, a man who is attacked every day by the media and by many on Capitol Hill, and he still makes progress. He will fight because he loves this country and wants every community to thrive. The question is, will we fight alongside him?

FIFTEEN

LET'S FIX THIS

22.1 million people in the United States "Not a U.S. Citizen."
—US Census report, September 2019

*65 percent of all border-crossers this year were either minors
or adults traveling with minors.*
—President Donald Trump, May 2019

*Every year, we admit 1.1 million immigrants as permanent
legal residents.*
—President Donald Trump, May 2019

Border Patrol agents, before we deported someone, would warn them to hide any cash they were carrying, because if they were stopped by cartels or Mexican police, they'd almost certainly steal the money.

In Phoenix, special agents were notified by Mexican police that a man we arrested was wanted in that country. We went through the proper processing procedures, and the man chose to voluntarily return. So we arranged to bring the prisoner and meet the Mexican authorities on a bridge at the port of entry.

Along with some Mexican police, the comandante of the Federal Judicial Police was there. We'll call him José. He gave me his business card and said (*en español*), "Thank you very much. This guy is wanted in our country. I appreciate your quick response."

Two months later, my wife and I and another couple were on our way to Baja, Mexico, for a few days of vacation. About an hour south of the border, we approached a military checkpoint with armed federales, the Mexican Federal Police. They pulled us over and started asking us a lot of questions, in fluent English. In between questions, they made quite a few comments to each other, in Spanish, including some crude and threatening remarks about the ladies. That was too much for me. I turned to the highest-ranking officer, who was interrogating us, and said (in his native language) that his comments were not acceptable and we would appreciate being treated with respect, especially since there were ladies in the car.

"You speak Spanish?" he asked, wide-eyed.

"Yes, I learned your language at the Border Patrol Academy." He wasn't happy about my linguistic skills or where I learned them.

After some tense exchanges, he said, "Everybody out of the car so we can search it."

"Fine," I shot back. "But could you do me one favor first?"

"What's that?"

"Call my friend, José, the comandante at the judicial police," I said, as I handed him José's business card.

Everyone froze.

"How, uh, how do you know him?" he stuttered.

"I arrested a fugitive a couple of months ago and turned him over to him. José told me if I ever needed anything in Mexico to be sure to call him. I think our treatment today was unprofessional. You're harassing us. We haven't violated any laws. I think this is a shakedown for cash."

With that and a few suspicious looks, we were on our way. North. Back home. I tried to look cool and collected, but that situation could have gone sideways in a hurry. Luckily, I remembered the commandant's name and had his card. Many aren't so lucky south of the border.

Let me be clear. This story, and every story in this book, is not a reflection on the average Mexican citizen or immigrant. I do blame corrupt Mexican cops, but I place more blame on state and federal politicians in Mexico, whose corruption has filtered down through an entire country.

Many in the Mexican government enable illegal immigration because, bottom line, it's a source of money for their economy—including the black-market economy. The leaders of those caravans don't walk through without greasing palms of certain law enforcement, military, and cartel members. The only reason Mexico has stepped up is because of the threat of tariffs and other economic "enticements." Mexico could do a lot more, and we should keep the pressure on them. What's really sad is that Mexico is now doing more to protect our sovereignty than our very own Congress. We cannot allow this to continue. Our national security should not have to rely on a few corrupt foreign government officials.

FIGHTING FOR THE TRUTH

You know the real story. We've exposed the lies. There is hope for our border and for our country. The crisis is immense, but the solutions are simple.

Before we talk details, let me make this crucial point. This isn't just my battle. It's your battle. We are in a struggle for the future of this country—a struggle for the rule of law, the right to defend our borders, and the ability to protect the citizens of this country. Honestly, I've never seen a crisis like this in my lifetime. How we respond to this struggle will not only define us but who we are as a nation.

You may have watched the impeachment scam of late 2019 and heard many Democrat leaders mouth the words, "No one is above the law, not even the president." Clearly, the president has not violated any law. He's actually insisted that the law be followed—in every capacity including immigration—unlike the Obama administration. But let's look at the hypocrisy of the Democrats' statement. They say no one is above the law and in the same breath proudly say, with words and actions, that illegal aliens *are* above the law. The same people who vilify ICE agents seem to forget about their oath to enforce the law and remove those who have been convicted of a crime in our courts. To Nancy Pelosi, Dick Durbin, Chuck Schumer, Alexandria Ocasio-Cortez, and the rest of the "open borders and abolish ICE" cartel—too many to name—*No one is above the law.* This principle shouldn't be a sound bite for your political campaigns. This is how the United States is supposed to operate: with liberty and justice for all.

This book has equipped you to join the fight, get involved, and confidently speak up. But, trust me, there will be pushback—even against what seems like common sense. So let's be clear about a few facts.

You and I are for a secure border because we want every American to enjoy a safe and peaceful community.

We know that respect for the law—and respect for law enforcement officers—is a cornerstone of the way of life we enjoy. Countries that don't have law and order have chaos, corruption, and injustice—which is why people flee those places. Making the United States a country that ignores laws, or selectively enforces them, doesn't help anyone. As I've said several times in this book, many people across the globe understandably want to be part of this country. We must stick with what makes us great.

The situation on our southern border truly is a crisis. Even though this president has made great advances and the numbers are currently down, the situation is still unacceptable. Drugs, crime, violence, and death are rampant. The legacy media doesn't report the facts. Cartels and gangs control northern Mexico, and nobody crosses without paying them or being abused by them. Illegal immigration is driven by human trafficking.

We may want or need more legal immigration as our economy continues to grow, but we must strive for zero illegal immigration. Being against illegal immigration does not make us anti-immigrant. But we need to acknowledge that our legal immigration system is outdated and dysfunctional—rewarding criminals while punishing those who follow the rules. Illegal employment is the chief enabler of illegal immigration.

Porous borders increase crime in the United States. Some studies show that ilegal aliens commit more crime than citizens per capita.

Legal immigration needs a merit-based system, as opposed to the current situation where everyone except US citizens gets to decide who immigrates here.

Walls work. Walls stop or slow down those who try to cross illegally—especially those smuggling drugs and human beings. You can't drive a truck over a wall.

Being against illegal immigration does not make a person racist. A majority of Hispanic citizens oppose illegal immigration. Those who scream "racist" do so because they don't have a reasonable excuse for fostering the crisis on the border. In 2019 a Marist/NPR/PBS poll asked, "Do you approve or disapprove of the job Donald Trump is doing as president?" Fifty percent of Latinos answered that they approved of his work as president.

The Border Patrol does not seek "family separation." The agency does its best to make sure every child is safe. Because of rampant fraud by human traffickers and the number of children who are abused by gangs and cartels, security is a top priority. "Zero tolerance" means we do not want one child to be harmed.

Sanctuary jurisdictions make life more dangerous for every member of the community, but especially for immigrants—legal and illegal. And these policies put our heroes at ICE at a greater risk of harm. Isn't their job dangerous enough?

ICE and other law enforcement agencies are under attack by Democrats. Instead of changing the law, those who want open borders choose to vilify American heroes who keep us safe. ICE goes after those with criminal records who have defied a judge's order. When you know the amount of drugs, especially opioids, that ICE has taken off our street, the thousands of violent criminals they've taken out of our communities, the number of children they saved from sexual predators, the number of women they rescued from sex traffickers, the numbers of weapons they have taken from cartels, you will agree that ICE is clearly in the business of protecting law-abiding people in this country—include those who despise them.

Current immigration laws and policies have loopholes as wide as Arizona. Fixing these would help us almost instantly regain control of our southern border and save countless lives of those who are enticed to put themselves into the hands of criminal cartels. If these loopholes are not fixed, more caravans will come, more women will be abused, and more children will die. Congress could easily address the root causes but has been unwilling to do so. We need Congress to make legal changes that will solidify the progress President Trump has made.

BORDER SECURITY

The first fix is obvious: Secure the border. Until we actually have a functioning border, every problem detailed in this book will continue to grow. We must:

- Increase funding for the Border Patrol, ICE, DHS, HHS, immigration courts, and Department of Defense.
- Keep building that wall, one section at a time.
- Keep pressuring Mexico—and other countries, including Guatemala, El Salvador, and Honduras—to keep migrants in their countries so asylum seekers can find safety more quickly. We've already sent over forty thousand migrants back into Mexico to wait for their hearing, and that's proven effective. But there are never-ending court challenges. If you really knew how much control the Mexican government has on our southern border, it would scare the daylights out of you.
- End the enticements to illegal immigration. When we reward certain behaviors, we'll get more of it. This applies to releasing detainees before their day in court, birthright citizenship, the ridiculously low bar for asylum claims, and the endless list of promised benefits—promised by Democrats but courtesy of you, the taxpayer.

ADDRESS THE TVPRA

The Victims of Trafficking and Violence Protection Act (TVPRA) was created in 2000 but subsequently renewed in 2003, 2006, and 2008. It was intended to combat trafficking of people into the sex trade and slavery. But the bad guys have figured out a way to use it as a free ticket to get into the United States.

If you are a child under the age of eighteen, a citizen of Mexico or Canada, and enter the US illegally, you will be screened to ascertain if you are a victim of trafficking. If you are, there are certain protections afforded you and you may get to reside in the country legally. However, if it is determined that you are not a victim of trafficking, you can easily and quickly be removed to your home country of Mexico or Canada—contiguous countries to the US. If you enter the US illegally and you are a citizen of any noncontiguous country, such as Guatemala, Honduras, or El Salvador, you cannot be removed quickly—even after it is proven that you are not a victim of trafficking. The processing of these cases can take years. This is the loophole within the TVPRA that causes so many unaccompanied alien children to be smuggled here, because they know they can't be easily removed, and they also know the US government will reunite them with parents, guardians, or sponsors in this country. Many never show up in court, and many have turned out to be gang members and criminals.

Congress can fix TVPRA in one day. Children of Central America need to be treated the same as children of Mexico and Canada. Again, the original intent of TVPRA—to protect victims of trafficking—was a good intention, but it is now being exploited. That isn't a theory or opinion; it's a fact.

THE FLORES SETTLEMENT AGREEMENT

The Flores settlement ended a lawsuit, Reno v. Flores, in 1993, and established rules to protect minor illegal alien children from being detained without "delay." The agreement has created giant loopholes, which are exploited by families and cartels who smuggle them. Congress needs to fix this agreement and legislate a permanent fix. ICE needs to detain family units in a family residential center, not a jail, long enough for them to see a judge and plead their case. Again, these facilities were built and designed for families. They look nothing like a jail. They are open-air campuses with first-rate medical care, pediatricians, dentists, child psychologists, school programs, law libraries, family visitation, educational programs for adults, and three meals a day with unlimited snacks. As a reminder, these facilities were approved, funded, built, and operated under the Obama administration. We housed illegal aliens long enough to see a judge—about forty days—in 2014 and 2015, and the process worked. Most lost their cases and were removed. Those who needed and deserved our protection were welcomed. The result? Illegal border crossings by families declined rapidly.

ASYLUM FOR THOSE WHO NEED IT

As we've shown with hard data, our asylum system is a joke—a cruel joke on those who truly need our protection and on US citizens who have no idea that nine out of ten claims are found to be frivolous.

In August 2019, the number of pending deportation cases in US immigration courts reached over 1 million, doubling in just over two years. And the average time it takes to try a case is two to five years, without appeals. While people claim asylum fraudulently and clog up the system with hundreds of thousands of cases, there are people in this world who are actually fleeing persecution from their governments—and they are stuck at the back of the line.

STOP ENTICING ILLEGAL CROSSINGS

When the US signals, through words and policy actions, that if you make it across our border and play the game, you can stay here for your entire life, do you think that increases or decreases the number of people willing to try? And do you think drug cartels increase or decrease activity when consequences for crossing illegally are eliminated? When members of Congress vow to "abolish ICE," does it embolden human traffickers?

Family groups continue to come because they are incentivized and rewarded to illegally enter our country. Those ordered deported ignore the rulings because there are no consequences. Court hearings are skipped because there are no penalties. They know ICE doesn't have the manpower to look for them all, and they know that half of Congress doesn't want them removed. We need criminal penalties for those defrauding this country's generosity.

BUILD THE BIG, BEAUTIFUL WALL

The wall is being built, where it needs to be built, based on input from the men and women on the front line.

If walls didn't work, the Left wouldn't be so triggered by them.

SANCTUARY CITIES

Congress needs to take action to make it unlawful for local jurisdictions to choose not to cooperate with federal law enforcement. They need to block sanctuary cities from receiving funding awarded by Department of Homeland Security (DHS). The Department of Justice needs to continue to push these appeals, all the way to the Supreme Court if necessary.

We must legislate the right of DHS to withhold SCAAP funding, which are federal funds sent to local jails to offset expenses of housing illegal inmates. Unbelievably, even if a jail refuses to cooperate with ICE, they can still receive federal assistance.

We also need to investigate the practice by some governors of pardoning illegal aliens—including convicted criminals—so they can't be deported.

Law enforcement must be shielded from Leftist lawsuits. If state or local law enforcement officers decide to honor detainment, they run the risk of being sued. This is insane and unacceptable. The federal government needs to indemnify them and protect them. We need to increase the number of cooperative agreements between local and state law enforcement agencies and ICE such as 287(g) agreements.

VISA OVERSTAYS

Visa fraud and overstays must stop. Knowingly overstaying a visa should be classified as a crime. It's estimated that 800,000 people per year overstay their visa, and we should bar violators from receiving any sort of immigration benefit for a certain period of time. Those who overstay their visa should be added to the National Crime Information Center database, so local law enforcement can know when someone is in this country illegally and take appropriate action.

Those who sponsor visas must also pass background checks and be verified to make sure they are not displacing legal workers already in the country. Those who apply for a visa already undergo significant background checks, but they should also pay a bond to encourage compliance.

ILLEGAL EMPLOYMENT

Require all employers to use E-Verify. Modify the program as I have outlined and make it mandatory. Done.

MERIT-BASED IMMIGRATION

The government of the United States is responsible for the security and prosperity of this country. We can't be the welfare provider for every poor country in the world. That might sound harsh, but it's the harsh reality.

I fully support the president's proposal on merit-based immigration, which is commonsense, pro-America, and compassionate.

Our current lack of standards has resulted in overcrowded schools, increased crime, overwhelmed hospitals and clinics, and huge strains on social services.

The visa lottery and "chain migration" simply do not serve the future of this country.

MY VISION FOR OUR COMMUNITIES

I don't think the life I enjoyed as a kid exists in most of America today. It's sad that kids can't get on their bike, go play until they hear the noon whistle, inhale lunch, and go back out without fear.

It's unfortunate that you can't feel safe driving in Mexico for a fishing trip. Ranchers on the southern border don't feel safe anymore because cartels run through their property every night. This should be the safest country in the world. You should feel protected. Your kids should feel safe. And we all should feel optimistic about our futures. Whether you have a ranch on the Rio Grande Valley or live on Long Island or in any big city, you should have that American dream.

We need elected officials who believe that, too. These solutions lead to an America we all want.

YOU ARE PART OF THE SOLUTION

The Left has marches and mantras. They have an agenda and they *know* they're right, even when faced with the facts about the border and illegal immigration. Democrats mobilize thousands on Capitol Hill.

Yes, many citizens stand up to defend and secure our border. But let's face it: We've been outnumbered and outmaneuvered in the public debate. Of course we don't want to mimic their hateful rhetoric and violence—and we don't need to in order to be effective.

We can expose lies with statistics and common sense. We can pressure leaders in our towns, states, and in Washington, DC. We can march. We can use social media to share facts, and we can write sensible letters to our elected officials and local newspapers. We can take a stand—with confidence—because we know that many Democrat policies—and *lack* of policies—actually harm everyone in this country in some way. We can speak boldly because we're not racist, heartless, or anti-immigrant.

If, God forbid, there is a crime in your community involving illegal aliens, raise hell about it—because we care about the victims. Ask candidates specific questions about policies, based on the material in this book. Support candidates who walk the walk. Demand a meeting with your representative and senator. Don't do what the Left does, in other words.

And, unlike me, try to keep your cool, okay?

You don't have to serve in the military to fight for our country. Citizens can fight for our country every day and in many ways. Don't remain quiet. Don't sit on the sidelines anymore. We're in the fight of our lives right now.

I can sum up this entire book with this sentiment: I want everyone in this country—in every community—to enjoy the America I enjoyed as a child.

We don't have to hear endless news stories about gang violence and illegal alien criminals. Border Patrol and ICE agents should not be fighting armies on our border and gangs in our cities. And they shouldn't have to fight elected officials. As I said in one of my recent appearances before Congress, I've never seen such hatred toward the men and women of ICE and the Border Patrol by our politicians than I have in the past three years. America deserves better.

Despite the violence and heartache I've seen in my career, I believe it's possible. The solutions are simple. If I'm not jaded, why should anyone be? Join me in this fight to elect those who will defend our country and pass laws to ensure America has a bright future. All my appearances before Congress prove two things: First, I really despise politics. Second, armed with just a few facts, any citizen can silence their hateful propaganda and expose power-hungry politicians who don't actually care about Americans—or immigrants.

Let's remind members of Congress: "You work for me!"

Let's remind members of law enforcement: "I'm thankful for you!"

THE WHITE HOUSE VISION

On May 16, 2019, President Trump unveiled his solutions to the immigration and border crisis. I include highlights here so you can see the clear vision we're striving to realize.

"This plan was not developed, I'm sorry to say, by politicians. It was designed with significant input from our great law enforcement professionals to detail what they need to make our border—which is 100 percent operationally secure."

[...]

"We must also restore the integrity of our broken asylum system. Our nation has a proud history of affording protection to those fleeing government persecutions. Unfortunately, legitimate asylum seekers are being displaced by those lodging frivolous claims—these are frivolous claims—to gain admission into our country. Asylum abuse also strains our public school systems, our hospitals, and local shelters, using funds that we should, and that have to, go to elderly veterans, at-risk youth, Americans in poverty,

and those in genuine need of protection. My plan expedites relief for legitimate asylum seekers by screening out the meritless claims. If you have a proper claim, you will quickly be admitted; if you don't, you will promptly be returned home."

[...]

"Crucially, our plan closes loopholes in federal law to make clear that gang members and criminals are inadmissible. These are some of the worst people anywhere in the world— MS-13 and others. And for criminals already here, we will ensure their swift deportation."

[...]

"A topic of less discussion in national media, but of vital importance to our country, is our legal immigration system itself. Our plan includes a sweeping modernization of our dysfunctional legal immigration process. It is totally dysfunctional. The system will finally be fair, transparent, and promote equality and opportunity for all. Every year, we admit 1.1 million immigrants as permanent legal residents. These green card holders get lifetime authorization to live and work here and a five-year path to American citizenship."

[...]

"The White House plan makes no change to the number of green cards allocated each year. But instead of admitting people through random chance, we will establish simple, universal criteria for admission to the United States. No matter where in the world you're born, no matter who your relatives are, if you want to become an American citizen, it

will be clear exactly what standard we ask you to achieve. This will increase the diversity of immigration flows into our country. We will replace the existing green card categories with a new visa, the Build America visa—which is what we all want to hear."

[…]

"Finally, to promote integration, assimilation, and national unity, future immigrants will be required to learn English and to pass a civics exam prior to admission. Through these steps, we will deliver an immigration system that respects, and even strengthens, our culture, our traditions, and our values."

[…]

"I had the honor of participating in a swearing-in ceremony for new Americans, right here in the Oval Office. It was a beautiful reminder that American citizenship is the most precious gift our nation has to offer. When we swear in new citizens, we do more than give them a permit; we give them a history, a heritage, a home, and a future of limitless possibilities and potential."

[…]

SECURING THE BORDER FIRST

Full border security is the bedrock of a functioning immigration system and it must come first.

- The crisis at our border is at a breaking point: Approximately 1 million aliens are projected to arrive at the border this year alone, and more than 100,000 aliens have arrived each of the past two months.

- The President's proposal establishes a self-sustaining and renewable border security fund that will:
  - Fully secure the border
  - Ensure 100 percent inspection of people and good at ports of entry
  - Stop drugs, contraband, and counterfeit goods
  - Facilitate faster trade
- The President['s] proposal will safeguard our homeland by continuing to add to the 400-plus miles of border wall underway in strategic locations. [. . .]
- The President's proposal will restore integrity to our broken asylum system and close legal loopholes to address the driving forces behind the humanitarian crisis at our southern border. [. . .]
  - The President's proposal will change the law to stop the flood of child smuggling and to rapidly reunite unaccompanied children with their families back home.
- Structural changes to immigration agencies will improve coordination and enforcement to combat longstanding problems, such as visa overstays.
- The President's proposal will ensure that all employees are legally authorized to work.

[. . .]

PRIORITIZING MERIT OVER CHANCE [. . .]

- Around 70 percent of the immigrants who come to the United States today are admitted based on family relationships or through the visa lottery.
  - The most vulnerable Americans are the ones hurt the most by the current system, which undercuts wages and drains our social safety net programs.

- The President's proposal creates the "Build America Visa," which will select immigrants based on a point system and features three high-skill categories:
    - Extraordinary talent
    - Professional and specialized vocations
    - Exceptional academic track records [. . .]
- Adopting the President's proposal will ensure prosperity and higher wages for all Americans—especially recent immigrants striving to achieve the American Dream. [. . .]
- The President's proposal will protect all workers from exploitation, fraud, and unlawful displacement.

[. . .]

THE GLOBAL RACE FOR TALENT [. . .]

- President Trump's proposal will move America to a more competitive and fair position of 57 percent employment and skill, 33 percent family, and 10 percent humanitarian.

JOIN ME IN THE FIGHT

Don't bother looking for me on social media. I don't tweet or post. But I hope you'll share facts from this book on those platforms.

If you'd like to join me in the fight and stay in touch, or have me speak at your event, please go to the website below and subscribe for email updates, so we can defend the border, save lives, and build strong communities—together.

www.TomHomanSpeaks.com

ACKNOWLEDGMENTS

This book was just the latest accomplishment in my long law enforcement career. To the publishing team at Hachette Book Group, thank you for your continued support. To my literary agent, Tom Winters, I so appreciate your belief in this message. To Mike Loomis, thank you for your guidance in helping me put my stories and motivation into words.

I want to thank my mom and dad for providing a loving home and always being there for their family. I miss them every day and know they're still watching over all seven children. Mom and Dad were always there for me, and continue to be to this day, through prayer. Thank you to my five sisters and brother. You are part of an amazing family, and your support for me has never diminished.

To the twin villages of Carthage and West Carthage, New York—the villages that raised me. To the hardworking men and women who lived a simpler life back then, but a life full of community spirit and caring for neighbors. I can't think of a better place on earth to be a kid, and I'll keep working so more kids can experience this type of loving community.

And finally, to my wife and children. For the sacrifices that you've made throughout my career, the missed first days of school, the missed birthdays and sporting events. For the anniversaries spent apart and the constant moves from town to town and state to state, in order for me to serve a larger role for this nation. For all the friends you left, for the many new schools, doctors, and churches. You had to bear the hate of those who hated me, including the protesters at our home and the terrible online attacks—dealing with those who threatened harm to you simply because you were my family. You supported what I've always stood for, and who I am. For all this and so much more, I thank and love you.

NOTES

CHAPTER 1: WHO I FIGHT FOR

Page 1: "Forced to flee Central America's Northern Triangle: A neglected humanitarian crisis," Médecins sans Frontières (Doctors Without Borders), May 2017. https://www.doctorswithoutborders.org/sites/default/files/2018-06/msf_forced-to-flee-central-americas-northern-triangle.pdf

4: Ralph Blumenthal, "Truck driver found guilty in deaths of 19 illegal immigrants in Texas in 2003," *New York Times*, November 6, 2006. https://www.nytimes.com/2006/12/05/world/americas/05iht-smuggle.3787320.html

6: Derek Hawkins, "San Antonio truck deaths recall horror of 19 who died in 2003 Texas smuggling case," *Washington Post*, July 24, 2017. https://www.washingtonpost.com/news/morning-mix/wp/2017/07/24/san-antonio-truck-deaths-recall-horror-of-19-who-died-in-2003-tex-smuggling-case

CHAPTER 3: THE REAL STORY ON OUR SOUTHERN BORDER

Page 53: Anna Giaritelli, "Most illegal crossings in 12 years: Border Patrol took 851,000 into custody during fiscal 2019," *Washington Examiner*, October 5, 2019. https://www.washingtonexaminer.com/news/most-illegal-crossings-in-12-years-border-patrol-took-851-000-into-custody-during-fiscal-2019

55: Melanie Arter, "HHS: Number of unaccompanied alien children entering US reaches highest in history," CNS News, September 19, 2019. https://www.cnsnews.com/news/article/melanie-arter/hhs-number-unaccompanied-minors-entering-us-reached-highest-history

CHAPTER 4: ANIMALS SMUGGLING HUMANS

Page 57: Paul Bedard, "Report: Illegal immigrant population inside US surged 550,000 in 2019," *Washington Examiner*, November 6, 2019. https://www.washingtonexaminer.com/washington-secrets/report-illegal-immigration-population-inside-us-surged-550-000-in-2019

57: Claire Hansen, "Immigration Court Case Backlog Hits 1 Million," *US News and World Report*, September 18, 2019. https://www.usnews.com/news/national-news/articles/2019-09-18/immigration-court-case-backlog-hits-1-million

61: "U.S. Border Patrol Nationwide Apprehensions by Citizenship and Sector in FY2007," US Customs and Border Protection, March 2019. https://www.cbp.gov/sites/default/files/assets/documents/2019-Mar/BP%20Apps%20by%20Sector%20and%20Citizenship%20FY07-FY18.pdf

CHAPTER 5: MAKE IMMIGRATION SAFE AND LEGAL AGAIN

Page 73: "Former national Hispanic leader found guilty of immigration fraud," Department of Justice, May 9, 1995. https://www.justice.gov/archive/opa/pr/Pre_96/May95/262.txt.html

77: "From the 9/11 hijackers to Amine El-Khalifi: Terrorists and the visa overstay problem," Hearing before the Subcommittee on Border and Maritime Security of the Committee on Homeland Security, House of Representatives, 112 Congress, US Government Publishing Office, March 6, 2012. https://www.govinfo.gov/content/pkg/CHRG-112hhrg76600/html/CHRG-112hhrg76600.htm

77: Jessica M. Vaughan and Preston Huennekens, "Analyzing the New Visa Overstay Report," Center for Immigration Studies, September 6, 2018. https://cis.org/Report/Analyzing-New-Visa-Overstay-Report

81: "President Donald J. Trump wants to fully secure our border and reform our immigration system to put America first," White House fact sheet, May 16, 2019. https://www.whitehouse.gov/briefings-statements/president-donald-j-trump-wants-to-fully-secure-our-border-and-reform-our-immigration-system-to-put-america-first

84: Caitlin Dickerson, "What is DACA? And how did it end up in the Supreme Court?" *New York Times*, November 12, 2019. https://www.nytimes.com/2019/11/12/us/daca-supreme-court.html

CHAPTER 6: ILLEGAL EMPLOYMENT: BIG PROBLEM, SIMPLE SOLUTIONS

Page 92: Michael Rubinkam, "Tree company Asplundh to pay record fine for immigration practices," *USA Today*, September 29, 2017. https://www.usatoday.com/story/money/2017/09/29/tree-company-asplundh-pay-record-fine-immigration-practices/715729001

93: "ICE worksite enforcement investigations in FY18 surge," US Immigration and Customs Enforcement, December 11, 2018. https://www.ice.gov/news/releases/ice-worksite-enforcement-investigations-fy18-surge

94: Jimmie E. Gates and Alissa Zhu, "ICE used ankle monitors, informants to plan immigration raids where 680 people were arrested," *USA Today*, August 10, 2019. https://www.usatoday.com/story/news/nation/2019/08/10/ice-raids-how-federal-investigation-led-mississippi-poultry-plants/1975583001

CHAPTER 7: ILLEGAL IMMIGRATION: FACTS, FEELINGS, AND FIXES

Page 99: Karen Zeigler and Steven A. Camarota, "67.3 million in the United States spoke a foreign language at home in 2018," Center for Immigration Studies, October 29, 2019. https://cis.org/Report/673-Million-United-States-Spoke-Foreign-Language-Home-2018

100: "Guatemala remittances—97 percent from USA: IOM Study," International Organization for Migration, February 17, 2017. https://www.iom.int/news/guatemala-remittances-97-percent-usa-iom-study

101: "Saliendo adelante: Why migrants risk it all," Creative Associates International, September 2019. http://www.creativeassociatesinternational.com/wp-content/uploads/2019/09/Migration-Study-Brief.pdf

101: "Myths vs facts about immigration proceedings," US Department of Justice, May 2019. https://www.justice.gov/eoir/page/file/1161001/download

102: "Migrant protection protocols," US Department of Homeland Security, January 24, 2019. https://www.dhs.gov/news/2019/01/24/migrant-protection-protocols

102: Adam Shaw, "Trump administration to expand 'Remain-in-Mexico' program at key border crossings," Fox News, November 22, 2019. https://www.foxnews.com/politics/trump-administration-to-strengthen-remain-in-mexico-in-key-areas-as-migrant-flows-adapt

108: "New estimate: 72,000 births annually to tourists, foreign students, and other visitors," Center for Immigration Studies, December 11, 2019. https://cis.org/Press-Release/Estimate-Births-Tourists-Foreign-Students-and-Other-Visitors

109: Jon Feere, "Birthright citizenship: Is it the right policy for America?" Center for Immigration Studies, April 29, 2015. https://cis.org/Birthright-Citizenship-it-Right-Policy-America

110: Benjamin Carlson, "Welcome to Maternity Hotel California," *Rolling Stone*, August 19, 2015. https://www.rollingstone.com/culture/culture-news/welcome-to-maternity-hotel-california-168813

112: Dyer Oxley, "Sheriff: Bob's Burgers robbery, assault a 'deliberate hoax,'" *Seattle PI*, November 5, 2019. https://www.seattlepi.com/news/crime/article/Sheriff-Bob-s-Burgers-robbery-assault-a-14810934.php

113: Steven A. Camarota and Karen Zeigler, "63% of non-citizen households access welfare programs," Center for Immigration Studies, November 20, 2018. https://cis.org/Report/63-NonCitizen-Households-Access-Welfare-Programs

114: Matt Pearce, "As Trump seeks reelection, immigrant voters stand in his path," *Los Angeles Times*, October 23, 2019. https://www.latimes.com/politics/story/2019-10-23/trump-attacks-immigrants-new-naturalized-citizen-voter-registration

CHAPTER 8: BLURRED BORDERS AND CRIME

Page 117: Mark Motivans, "Immigration, Citizenship, and the Federal Justice System, 1998–2018," US Department of Justice, August 2019. https://www.bjs.gov/content/pub/pdf/icfjs9818.pdf

119: "Remarks by President Trump to Law Enforcement Officials on MS-13," White House, July 28, 2017. https://www.whitehouse.gov/briefings-statements/remarks-president-trump-law-enforcement-officials-ms-13

126: Luis Noe-Bustamante, Antonio Flores, and Sono Shah, "Facts on Hispanics of Salvadoran origin in the United States, 2017," Pew Research Center, September 16, 2019. https://www.pewresearch.org/hispanic/fact-sheet/u-s-hispanics-facts-on-salvadoran-origin-latinos

131: Beth Warren, "El Mencho's American empire: Mexican drug lord's super cartel infiltrates U.S. small towns," *USA Today*, November 24, 2019. https://www.usatoday.com/in-depth/news/crime/2019/11/24/el-menchos-mexican-drug-cartel-cjng-empire-devastating-small-towns/4181733002

132: "Departments of Justice and Homeland Security release quarterly alien incarceration report highlighting the negative effects of illegal immigration and the need for border security," US Department of Justice, June 7, 2018. https://www.justice.gov/opa/pr/departments-justice-and-homeland-security-release-quarterly-alien-incarceration-report

136: Eric Kirkwood, "New York green-light law creates serious and unprecedented hurdles for immigration enforcement," Center for Immigration Studies, November 25, 2019. https://cis.org/Report/New-York-GreenLight-Law-Creates-Serious-and-Unprecedented-Hurdles-Immigration-Enforcement

136: "U.S. Immigration and Customs Enforcement Fiscal Year 2019 Enforcement and Removal Operations Report," US Immigration and Customs Enforcement, 2019. https://www.ice.gov/sites/default/files/documents/Document/2019/eroReportFY2019.pdf

CHAPTER 9: BUILD THOSE WALLS

Page 139: "U.S. Border Patrol Southwest Border Apprehensions by Sector FY2018," US Customs and Border Protection, October 23, 2018. https://www.cbp.gov/newsroom/stats/usbp-sw-border-apprehensions

148: Matt O'Brien and Spencer Raley, "The Fiscal Burden of Illegal Immigration on United States Taxpayers," Federation for American Immigration Reform, September 27, 2017. https://www.fairus.org/issue/publications-resources/fiscal-burden-illegal-immigration-united-states-taxpayers

CHAPTER 10: ARE BORDERS RACIST?

Page 153: Matt Finn, "Chicago police instructs officers to not cooperate with DHS, memo shows: 'Sickening what's happening,'" Fox News, September 30, 2019. https://www.foxnews.com/us/chicago-police-dont-cooperate-dhs-immigration

157: "Office for Civil Rights and Civil Liberties," US Department of Homeland Security. https://www.dhs.gov/office-civil-rights-and-civil-liberties and https://www.dhs.gov/data-complaints-received

158: Ronn Blitzer, "Rashida Tlaib, in contentious tour, tells Detroit police chief to hire only black analysts for facial recognition program," Fox News, October 2, 2019. https://www.foxnews.com/politics/rashida-tlaib-tells-detroit-police-chief-only-black-people-should-be-hired-to-use-facial-recognition-software

CHAPTER 11: ZERO TOLERANCE AND THE FALLACY OF "FAMILY SEPARATION"

Page 161: Kate Sullivan, "Record 14,000 unaccompanied immigrant children in US custody, HHS confirms," CNN, November 23, 2018. https://www.cnn.com/2018/11/23/politics/hhs-record-14000-immigrant-children-us-custody/index.html

164: Nicholas Ballasy, "Former ICE director to AOC: U.S. citizens who commit crimes get separated from their families," PJ Media, July 13, 2019. https://pjmedia.com/trending/former-ice-director-to-aoc-u-s-citizens-who-commit-crimes-get-separated-from-their-families

CHAPTER 12: SANCTUARY FOR CRIMINALS

Page 177: "Sanctuary Cities," Center for Immigration Studies, November 7, 2018. https://cis.org/Fact-Sheet/Sanctuary-Cities

183: Vandana Rambaran, "Maryland sanctuary county rolls back anti-ICE policy after multiple illegal immigrants are accused of rape," Fox News, November 5, 2019. https://www.foxnews.com/us/maryland-sanctuary-county-rolls-back-anti-ice-policy-after-multiple-illegal-immigrants-charged-with-rape

184: Morgan Phillips, "ICE slams Maryland county officials after release of illegal immigrant accused of child molestation," Fox News, November 9, 2019. https://www.foxnews.com/us/ice-slams-maryland-officials-for-releasing-undocumented-alleged-child-molester

186: "Immigration and Nationality Act," US Citizenship and Immigration Services. https://www.uscis.gov/legal-resources/immigration-and-nationality-act

188: "Acting ICE director calls out jurisdictions with sanctuary policies for threatening public safety," US Immigration and Customs Enforcement, September 26, 2019. https://www.ice.gov/news/releases/acting-ice-director-calls-out-jurisdictions-sanctuary-policies-threatening-public

190: Stephen Dinan, "Los Angeles' sanctuary policy releases 100 criminals a day: ICE," *Washington Times*, October 22, 2019. https://www.washingtontimes.com/news/2019/oct/22/las-sanctuary-policy-releases-100-criminals-day-ic

CHAPTER 13: THE WAR AGAINST ICE

Page 195: Lisa Rein, "Meet the man the White House has honored for deporting illegal immigrants," *Washington Post*, April 25, 2016. https://www.washingtonpost.com/news/powerpost/wp/2016/04/25/meet-the-man-the-white-house-has-honored-for-deporting-illegal-immigrants

200: Anna Giaritelli, "Florida headquarters of private immigrant detention center company vandalized by activists," *Washington Examiner*, December 3, 2019. https://www.washingtonexaminer.com/news/florida-headquarters-of-private-immigrant-detention-center-company-vandalized-by-activists

202: "Pelosi statement on Trump administration ICE raids targeting the San Francisco Bay Area," February 28, 2018. https://www.speaker.gov/newsroom/22818

204: Stephen Dinan, "Fairfax County cancels suspension, restores officer who cooperated with ICE," *Washington Times*, October 2, 2019. https://www.washingtontimes.com/news/2019/oct/2/fairfax-county-police-officer-suspended-ice-cooper

CHAPTER 14: THE TRUMP EFFECT

Page 213: "Southwest Border Migration FY2017," US Customs and Border Protection. https://www.cbp.gov/newsroom/stats/sw-border-migration-fy2017

230: Adam Shaw, "As Trump administration confronts migrant crisis, detention centers are clearing out," Fox News, November 27, 2019. https://www.foxnews.com/politics/trump-migrant-detention-centers

232: "NPR/PBS NewsHour/Marist Poll Results," Marist Poll, January 17, 2019. http://maristpoll.marist.edu/npr-pbs-newshour-marist-poll-results-2

INDEX

ABOUT THE AUTHOR

TOM HOMAN is from northern New York State. He holds an associate degree in criminal justice from Jefferson Community College and a bachelor's degree from SUNY Polytechnic Institute.

He served as a police officer in West Carthage, New York, before joining the United States Border Patrol in 1984. Homan served as a Border Patrol agent, investigator, special agent, supervisor special agent, assistant director of investigations, assistant special agent in charge, deputy special agent in charge, and special agent in charge before being named executive associate director of ICE at headquarters in Washington, DC, during the Obama administration in 2013.

Homan was appointed acting director of Immigration and Customs Enforcement (ICE) on January 30, 2017, by President Donald Trump and later nominated to that position by President Trump in November 2017. He subsequently retired in June 2018. He started at the bottom rung of the law enforcement ladder in 1984 and made it to the top rung in 2017, without missing a single rung. Homan was the first ICE director who came up through the ranks, his proudest career accomplishment.

In 2015 President Obama gave Homan the highest professional award possible, the Distinguished Presidential Rank Award, for his exemplary leadership and extensive accomplishments in the area of immigration enforcement. He also was awarded the Distinguished Service Medal in 2018 by the Trump administration in recognition of exceptionally distinguished and transformational service to strengthen homeland security for the United States. Also in 2018 he was awarded the Law Enforcement Person of the Year Award from the Federal Law Enforcement Officers Association, which represents over twenty-six thousand federal law enforcement officers. In November 2019, Homan received the Man of the Year Award from *Blue* Magazine, a law enforcement publication created by and managed by law enforcement career professionals.